Reviewing masterful work by Nirjhar was similar to taking an expansion course in a technical field where my colleagues and I have had a great deal of experience. The exposure to digital transformation is expressed very well in written texts. Nirjhar has demonstrated those concepts with some very clever illustrations as well, which will allow the reader to link the emerging digital ideas with the well-established traditional processes. We found this particularly effective in the discussion of transforming established digital systems to high-speed 5G digital systems. In the highly competitive market, digital transformation is not only advantageous but mandatory. Nirjhar has meticulously highlighted the philosophy and architecture of digital transformation with excellent writing and frequent illustrations.

The explanations of the essential changes required have provided us with an excellent guidebook on counselling our clients. Also, it has given us knowledge for improving the design, architecture, and equations we use in our current systems.

I enjoyed reading the book. Even though we are changing from current heritage systems to higher speeds, there are infinite growth prospects for digital analysis and communication. This book is a superb prelude to that eventuality.

–**Dr. David G. Halloran,** *Chairman, Halloran Associates, Florida, USA*

In the digital age, digital challenges are growing each day. Nirjhar's book brings up relevant topics of today's fast-changing world. This book will help industries to cope with the new settings and learn to function in Industry 4.0.

This book is a great starting point and helpful for readers to understand many of the problems and concepts the business world deals with daily. The book explains digital transformation by using a logical train of thought. Nirjhar has in-depth knowledge and insight that shows throughout the book.

Whether you are at a beginner level or an experienced scholar in digital transformation, this book will be helpful for you.

–**Alexandra C.M. Katzian,** *Undergraduate Research Fellow*
*Kirchliche Pädagogische Hochschule Wien/Krems, Austria*

Nirjhar's book on Digital Transformation is very resourceful for any company trying to adopt digital transformation as a journey and they can add this book into their inventory for their employees and managers as a reference. This book gives a thorough systematic process with steps that a company can prepare for before entering this transformation journey. Nirjhar has done a phenomenal job by collecting all data points related to the subject. This book reflects his knowledge and research works in the subject. I highly recommend this book to anyone trying to gather knowledge in this subject.

−**Anuradha Chattaraj,** *Senior Director, Verisk Analytics*
*Jersey City, NJ, USA*

Nirjhar's book on Digital Transformation is a delightful guide, full of important information and illustrations for those of us who want to know about digital transformation processes. With the proliferation of digital and mobile technologies, it is the right time to learn about digital transformation. Strategic understanding of digital transformation is essential for all students and professionals irrespective of their field of work. What is the need for digital tools, how can it be implemented, and what are the essential elements for digital transformation? Nirjhar's book is the answer to all these queries. The most important part of the book is the digital vision and strategy that is mentioned meticulously. Nirjhar has written a must-read guide for anyone who likes to know about digital transformation.

−**Dr. Apurba Shee,** *Associate Professor of Applied Economics*
*Natural Resources Institute, University of Greenwich, United Kingdom*

# Digital Transformation

# Digital Transformation

## A Strategic Structure for Implementation

Nirjhar Chakravorti

Routledge
Taylor & Francis Group

A PRODUCTIVITY PRESS BOOK

First published 2022
by Routledge
605 Third Avenue, New York, NY 10158

and by Routledge
4 Park Square, Milton Park, Abingdon, Oxon, OX14 4RN

*Routledge is an imprint of the Taylor & Francis Group, an informa business*

ISBN: 978-1-032-22021-5 (hbk)
ISBN: 978-1-032-22019-2 (pbk)
ISBN: 978-1-003-27090-4 (ebk)

DOI: 10.4324/9781003270904

Typeset in Minion
by MPS Limited, Dehradun

# Contents

Acknowledgments.................................................................. ix
Author................................................................................ xi
Introduction: Let's Grow Digitally ..................................... xiii

**Chapter 1**  Digital Transformation Overview............................1

**Chapter 2**  Digital Challenges for Industries .........................5

      2.1   Exponential Growth .........................................5
      2.2   Deconstruction of Value Chain ....................9
      2.3   Disruption and Incumbency Factor...........11
      2.4   Economies .....................................................13

**Chapter 3**  Applicability of Digital Transformation............ 15

**Chapter 4**  Digital Transformation Framework ................. 23

      4.1   Strategy .........................................................23
      4.2   Key Enabler....................................................27
      4.3   Digital Duality...............................................31
      4.4   Ambidexterity................................................35
      4.5   Two-Speed IT.................................................39
      4.6   Governance and Funding..............................41

**Chapter 5**  People and Organization Structure................... 43

      5.1   Agility Trio .....................................................43
      5.2   Structure.........................................................47
      5.3   Agile Scale......................................................49

**Chapter 6** Capability Delivery Activities ................................................. 57

      6.1    Process Delivery .............................................................. 57

      6.2    Enabler Delivery ............................................................. 65

**Chapter 7** Life Cycle Benefits .................................................... 93

      7.1    Life Cycle Benefits of Strategic Structure
             Components ................................................................. 94

References ............................................................................... 97
Index ...................................................................................... 103

# Acknowledgments

I am immensely grateful to Dr. Promode Ranjan Bandyopadhay, an eminent scientist from the United States for his valuable advice.

I would like to express my gratitude to Dr. David Halloran, Chairman and Founder of Halloran Associates, Florida, United States for encouragement.

I am sincerely thankful to Dr. Amaresh Dalal, Professor, IIT Guwahati, India for his support.

I would like to express my thankfulness to Ms. Anuradha Chattaraj, Senior Director at Verisk Analytics, New Jersey, United States for her valuable time.

I would like to express gratitude to Dr. Apurba Shee, Associate Professor of Applied Economics, Natural Resources Institute, University of Greenwich, United Kingdom for encouragement.

I am thankful to Alexandra C.M. Katzian, Undergraduate Research Fellow at Kirchliche Pädagogische Hochschule Wien/Krems, Austria for her suggestions.

I am sincerely grateful to Business Strategist, Claire Oatway and Agile Coach, Samik Mukherjee for their valuable opinions.

I would like to express my appreciation to Dr. Tapan Choudhury, President, Tata Consulting Engineers Limited for his inspiration.

I am sincerely thankful to Sushil Rawat, Kaustav Das and S.L. Bandyopadhyay of Tata Consulting Engineers Limited for their encouragement.

I am grateful to Dr. Sukumar Pati, Assistant Professor, NIT, Silchar, India for his valuable suggestions.

I am grateful to Dr. Amitava Ray, Principal, Jalpaiguri Government Engineering College, India for his advice.

I am thankful to my personal guides Prof. Basudeb Ghoshal, Amal Kumar Sil, Binoy Krishna Mistry and Dr. S.K. De for their encouragement.

I would like to provide special thanks to my friends Sanat Adhikary, Rajib Bhattacharya, Ramu Chalumuri, Amy Bruton Bailey and George Bailey who supported me to complete the book.

I would like to express my gratitude to my wife, Shipra Roy Chowdhury, my daughters Samriddhi and Souriti and all my family members for their constant support.

# Author

**Nirjhar Chakravorti** was born and raised in the small historical town of Murshidabad in the eastern part of India. Growing up, he was fascinated by football, and that interest led to early exposure to structured thinking and leadership skills in a team game. During his graduation days, Nirjhar spent time with nature in the foothills of the Himalayas. Nirjhar completed his graduation in Mechanical Engineering in Y2K. Initially a mechanical design engineer, he has experienced many changes in his career path that includes project engineering and management, total productive maintenance, cost estimation, life cycle cost analysis and asset integrity management. Throughout his life, he has been a leader and influencer. His varied exposure has helped him develop ideas.

In his various roles in life, he realized that the world around us is transforming rapidly due to digital applications. During his stay in Wales (United Kingdom) in 2020, Nirjhar developed his ideas for strategic implementation of the digital transformation process.

# Introduction: Let's Grow Digitally

Digital transformation is the process of embracing digital technologies for services and businesses. Digital transformation is not simply about adopting digital technologies. It is a process of making multidimensional changes to provide value-added, customer-centric services.

Today, the importance of digital transformation is well known. But there is doubt about the logic behind the adoption of digital transformation. What type of organization can embrace it, how to implement it and what activities need to be carried out to adopt digital transformation? There is not enough clarity. There is also doubt about people and organizational skills.

This book illustrates a strategic structure that is useful for adopting digital transformation. The objective of strategic structure is to provide methodical guidance to understand and implement the digital transformation process in an organization. The strategic structure is for business owners, executives and managers. This is also for future industry leaders who want to empower themselves with digital transformation knowledge. The book will encourage social workers, public sector officers and legislators to learn about the strategy for digital transformation. It is for students and academics as well because the education system is changing rapidly to deal with the digital transformation. This book is written in such a way that people with a non-digital background can generate an overall concept on the entire digitalization process.

Keep in mind that there is no formal beginning for digital transformation. Maybe your organization is participating in the process, knowingly or unknowingly. Because, in the current scenario, it is almost impossible to continue living without it. To get the most out of digitalization and succeed in the current digital age, make a conscious decision following the strategic structure.

Let's be part of the digital revolution. Let's take a journey into the future, enlightened by the digital transformation process.

**Nirjhar Chakravorti**

# 1

## Digital Transformation Overview

With the advent of digital technologies, society is reshaping itself radically. In the last decade, digital technologies have brought fundamental changes in the industry and business environment. The holistic socioeconomic and industrial changes are a result of general-purpose technology aspects of digital transformation. Transformations due to general-purpose technologies are rare and have inherent capabilities of self-transformation to create long-term benefits across the entire global business environment. After steam engine, electricity generator and printing press, the recent development of digital transformation has created an opportunity with extensive sustainable and incremental influence for disruption and renovation. However, the most important difference between digital transformation and the previous general-purpose technologies such as steam engine and electric generator is the pace at which technology is being penetrated across the globe. To cope with the accelerated speed of global digitalization, the digital transformation process should be accepted, adopted and adapted across society and business.

Digital transformation has also reshaped the concept of business competitiveness and it influenced industry models to focus on the business ecosystem. The interactive economic community-based approach of the business ecosystem evolved due to the advent of digital technologies. The business ecosystems are the multidimensional dynamic matrix of entities networking with each other to generate and exchange maintainable value for all the participants. With the rapid growth of digital transformation, the concept of the business ecosystem is becoming more powerful where competition is getting replaced by the idea of co-opetition. With this changing dynamic, pursuing digital transformation

DOI: 10.4324/9781003270904-1

is becoming important for organizations to sustain and flourish in the complex business ecosystem.

For enhancing customer experience and meeting fast-changing business needs, digital transformation enables an organization to transform the culture and way of working. Digital technologies such as big data, cloud, Internet of Things (IoT), Additive Manufacturing and Artificial Intelligence (AI) are creating immense value to organizations. The application of these technologies is not limited to any specific sector such as telecommunication services or information technology, rather it creates value across the industry. The discrete and process manufacturing sector has also started adopting emerging technologies like cloud and IoT. Investment in digital transformation is increasing globally across the business sectors. These investments show that every business sector, including manufacturing industries, has identified the importance of digital application and is implementing digital transformation.

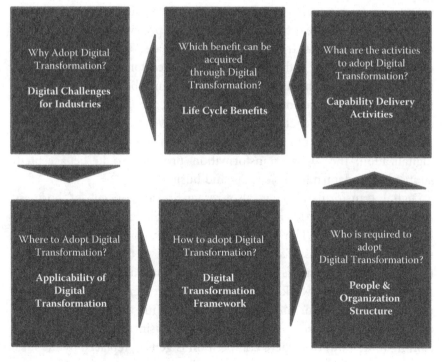

**FIGURE 1.1**
Strategic Structure for Digital Transformation

To conceive and adopt digital transformation in an organization, a strategic structure, as illustrated in Figure 1.1, is a useful guideline. The strategic structure consists of six subject groups, such as Digital Challenges for Industries, Applicability of Digital Transformation, Digital Transformation Framework, People and Organization Structure, Capability Delivery Activities and Life Cycle Benefits.

# 2

## Digital Challenges for Industries

Due to digital technologies, the world is transforming very fast. To cope with the changing business environment, driven by the concept of Industry 4.0, all businesses including the manufacturing sector have also started the digital transformation. Digital technologies are the enabler for Industry 4.0 Revolution. Adopting change is not an easy decision for an organization. Digital transformation, with its very nature of the soft application, is oriented toward services. On the contrary, the manufacturing sector deals with products and materials. It is not easy to conceive the manufacturing sector business as services. Naturally, regarding investment for digital transformation, there is a decision-making dilemma in the manufacturing sectors. All other sectors, as well, have reservations regarding the extent to which digital platforms should be adopted. To overcome these dilemmas, there is a need for a balanced understanding of the digital transformation that will enable organizations, including the manufacturing sector, to arrive at a conscious decision. Also, it is necessary for organizations to identify various aspects that influence businesses in the digital era, such as exponential growth, deconstruction of the value chain, disruptions and business economies (Figure 2.1).

## 2.1 EXPONENTIAL GROWTH

One of the most important things that makes digital transformation unique is the speed of change, which is commonly referred to as exponential growth.

DOI: 10.4324/9781003270904-2                                                                5

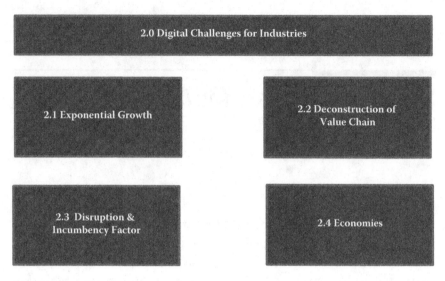

**FIGURE 2.1**
Digital Challenges for Industries

Everyday, normal human beings interact with lots of information or data. As per a study, humans receive 11 million pieces of information in one second, however, only 40 pieces of information can be processed by the brain. Therefore, it is a huge waste of information compared to information gained. That is the reason, normally the human mind is more processed with a linear way of thinking. For example, the human mind is more tuned to understand a growth series of 2, 3, 4, 5, 6, 7, 8, 9, 10 and so on. However, conceiving exponential growth is normally beyond the capacity of human imagination. For example, the series 2, 4, 8, 16, 32, 64, 128, 256, 512 and so on, is a growth series where each number is multiplied by 2 (Figure 2.2).

Digital technologies are evolving at an exponential pace, which is beyond the imagination of human understanding. Lack of understanding of the exponential growth of digital technologies is one of the major reasons for the dilemma that the majority of business organizations are facing, especially the manufacturing sector. The understanding of the exponential nature of digital growth may be helpful to make appropriate business decisions.

Three fundamental laws are useful to provide clarity about the exponential growth of digital technology.

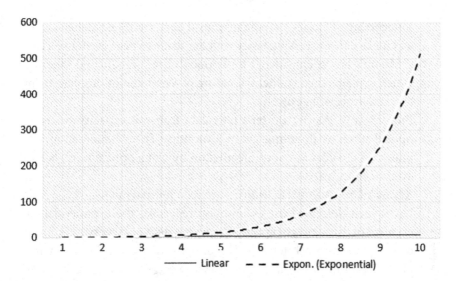

**FIGURE 2.2**
Linear and Exponential Growth

- *Moore's Law*: Gordon Moore's law regarding processing power is one of the most significant observations to describe the exponential growth of digital technology. In 1965, he observed that, since its inception in 1959, the number of components on an integrated circuit would almost doubling every year. It was later modified that; the doubling phenomenon was occurring every 18 months. This observation signifies that every 18 months, the computer would have twice as much processing power, due to shrinking the dimension on an integrated structure. Due to this scaling phenomenon, chip functionality improved exponentially with time with a constant cost per generation. Moore's observation remained true for the next 40 years which caused a huge positive technological and eventually social impact. But the nature of the shrinking dimension came to an end as 2D lithography capability approached the atomic scale.

  To overcome this issue of shrinking dimension, there are various alternative options, such as Denser Packaging (e.g. Chip Staking in 3D Using through Silicon Via), Advanced Materials (e.g. Tunneling Field-Effect Transistor, Strained Silicon, Carbon Nanotubes, etc.), computer architecture (e.g. advanced circuit design, Dark Silicon, etc.), Reducing Resistance (e.g. Crystalline Metals), a new way of storing and transferring of bits (e.g. topological insulators, etc.). These alternatives will make data processing faster with the advancement of Moore's law.

Moore's law is considered to be one of the fundamental theories, which explains the exponential nature of technological improvement for data processing power.

- *Butter's Law*: As per Butter's law, data transmit capacity by using optical fibres is doubling every 9 months. This phenomenon implies that the cost of data transmission by using optical fibre, is half every 9 months.

- *Kryder's Law*: In 2005, *Scientific American* journal published Kryder's Law which described the assumption regarding the exponential increment of data storage capacity. As per Kryder's law, every 13 months, disk density or areal density will be doubled. One of the major implications of this assumption will lower storage expenditure.

There is an argument that Kryder's Law is based on generalization. However, it provides a reasonable understanding of the trend of data storage capacity.

These three laws are important because they deal with significant areas related to data: processing, communicating and storing. As per these laws, there is exponential growth in all the areas related to data processing, communicating and storing, which ultimately lead to better digital services at rapidly reducing cost. It is a fact that the cost of digitally advanced equipment is reducing at a fast rate. For example, the cost of a top-of-the-range drone has reduced from $100,000 in 2007 to $500 in 2015. There are other theories as well, such as Rose's Law which is expected to cause radical changes in the digital world.

Information and, more precisely, data are one of the most important entities for any organization, irrespective of the nature of product or services and modus operandi. Proper collection, storage, process and communication of data within and outside an organization are useful to make appropriate decisions for different purposes and levels. These are the keys to success for an organization, which is true for any business including the manufacturing sector. The manufacturing sector is the biggest user of data. With digital technologies, the importance of data is becoming more visible. For example, tracking manufacturing data, cloud computing and the Internet of Things (IoT) help the manufacturer. To observe production and labor time trends, rectify quality and maintenance issues and minimize various safety and business-related risks, data-driven manufacturing plays an important role. The manufacturing team receives more actionable information through proper collection and communication of data, which makes the system more efficient. Making use of data helps manufacturers to identify irregularities and rectify them in a very short period which enhances consistency. Data supports manufacturers in developing new products and processes. In any business, proper handling of data has multiple importance. Due to the exponential growth of digital technologies, various new data-handling tools and techniques are emerging quickly which has the potential to change the business context. Businesses that can successfully adopt and enhance their data-handling capabilities in conducting business operations can place themselves ahead of competitors. More importantly, businesses that cannot foresee the implication of rapidly increasing digital technologies or that fail to effectively implement digital transformation will eventually lag the competition.

## 2.2 DECONSTRUCTION OF VALUE CHAIN

The purpose of any industry is to transform raw input into a market-ready product or service. The major player involved in this transformation process are suppliers, producers and distributors. This is applicable for any industry which includes the manufacturing sector. As per traditional business architecture, in every industry, over the period, each producer used to create their own vertically integrated value chain with a given set of suppliers and distributors to create value from the system for serving the end user (Figure 2.3). The purpose of creating a given set of suppliers, producers and distributors is to help the players communicate within the value chain with set parameters and save time and money to explore a new market. It helps to serve customers effectively, as the flow of information within a value chain is easier. More efficient is the vertical stack, more efficient is the organization. One of the major drivers for creating a vertical stack is the flow of information, as effective processing, communicating and storing information and data are crucial and involve time, money and risks.

With the advent of digital transformation, the link between players within the value chain is becoming weaker, because collecting, storing, processing and communicating information and data are becoming much easier, faster

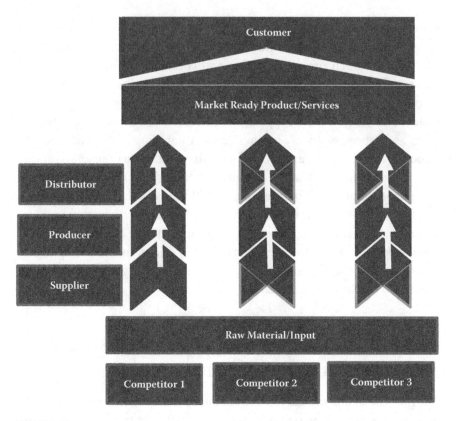

**FIGURE 2.3**
Traditional Vertically Stacked Value Chain

and cheaper. For example, if a steel fabricator suddenly needs extra steel plates of a certain grade and thickness, they need not rely upon and wait for their traditional suppliers; rather they can use any online supply chain portal and globally search for the material with various options. The portal itself will compare the options and provide the best available deal, which the fabricator can order straightway using the portal. Naturally, this phenomenon is breaking the traditional vertically integrated value chain and allowing horizontal interaction among the players with a more cooperative, but competitive business ecosystem. This phenomenon allows the creations of a horizontal stack at different levels, based on the players' adaptation of digital technologies (Figure 2.4). The player with a stronger digital platform will be more effective in the global business ecosystem.

With the deconstruction of the traditional value chain, new business models are evolving that focus on the desegregation of information flow

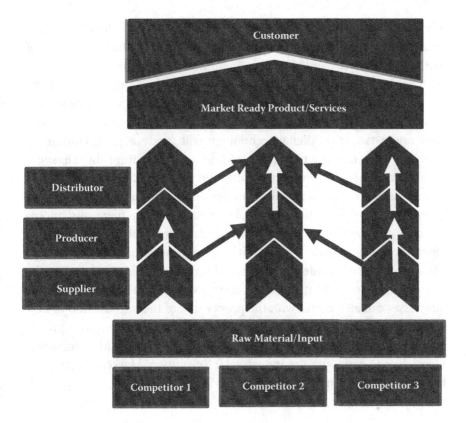

**FIGURE 2.4**
Modern Horizontally Stacked Value Chain Based on a Digital Platform

and physical material flow. This will eventually lead to an effective business environment with customer empowerment. In this scenario, relying on the traditional vertically stacked business model is becoming a liability for the incumbent businesses. By leveraging existing capabilities, the faster adaptation of a new business model based on a digital platform is crucial for the sustenance of an existing business.

## 2.3 DISRUPTION AND INCUMBENCY FACTOR

With the exponential growth of digital application, the traditional business value chain is disintegrating, and the incumbent businesses are being disrupted by digital technology-driven approaches. What does disruption mean? Disruption is the action of holistic change of the traditional way of work of industry by utilizing new methodology or technology. As per a 2018 report, 93 per cent of executives feel that their industry is will be disrupted in the coming 5 years, however, only 20 per cent believe that they are adequately prepared to face the disruption. Even though executives understand that digital technology will create a good amount of change to the market, they lack confidence in adopting digitalization. Because most people believe that disruption is unpredictable, and it occurs by chance. Also, there is a general understanding that a disruptive force is going to occupy the entire market. However, these are mere misconceptions as disruption can be predictably addressed with proper strategy. Disruption brings new opportunities and innovation to the market. Various new players enter the market with innovative ideas to disrupt the existing industry. But at the same time, existing legacy and incumbent businesses can also evolve with the proper mix of the introduction of new ideas and utilization of existing infrastructures. For example, with proper adaptation of digital technologies, manufacturing companies can uplift themselves to cope with the Industry 4.0 Revolution. Market disruption is not a new phenomenon. It occurred previously at various levels, such as at the product level or process level or industry level. But Industry 4.0 has special significance as it will affect all sectors in industries and cause a holistic socioeconomic change. The scale factor of change across the industry is also highly noticeable. That is the reason it is called a revolution. The world has experienced industry-level changes previously as well, with First, Second and Third Industrial Revolutions (Figure 2.5).

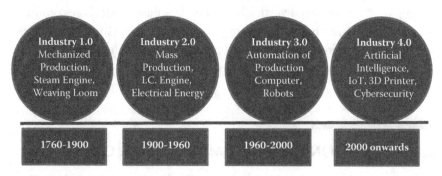

**FIGURE 2.5**
Industrial Revolutions

In the past, the world faced disruption during previous revolutions, which eventually added value to industries and people's lives. Similarly, industries can cope with Industry 4.0 by adopting digital technologies to suit their business needs. There are two parts, one is not to ignore digital technology, and two, while implementing digital transformation, adopt a proper strategy to suit the business objective. For incumbent companies, the legacy structure is not a liability, rather it is a benefit. Utilize and reinforce the existing capabilities for digital transformation.

## 2.4 ECONOMIES

Global wisdom has already acknowledged that there is no scope of going back by escaping the digital transformation process. Already businesses across the industry started investing or planning to invest in digital technologies. But still, there is a dilemma in many sections, especially regarding economic benefit against the investment and a few other concerns such as unemployment due to automation and political consequences. Also, there is debate over the productivity growth rate by introducing digital technologies. In this context, many people refer to Nobel laurate Robert Solow's famous remark that we see computers everywhere, but in the productivity statistics. This is famously known as Solow's Paradox. Adaptation of digital transformation is a complex process that requires a holistic change of business model. Implementation of the process is expensive and time-consuming. Is there a recognizable and sustainable economic benefit to be gained from digital transformation? Is the huge investment in digital technology worthy for businesses? As per a 2020 Global Survey Report, 22 per cent of manufacturing and industrial companies were recognized as champions (for the period between 2017 and 2019) that invested about 39 per cent of their total revenue for digital application and enjoyed a revenue gain of 27 per cent, whereas the remaining 78 per cent of companies in the sample invested about 26 per cent of their total revenue in digital transformation with a revenue gain of about 7 per cent. As per the survey, the champions invested 1.5 times of their total revenue in digital transformation and enjoyed four times higher revenue gain than the rest of the companies in the sample. According to another 2018 market research data, companies realized productivity growth and revenue over the past decades.

However, this growth was unevenly distributed, because it was driven by a small group of industry leaders. Who are the industry leaders? Industry leaders are referred to as the top 20 per cent of companies by productivity in each industry. The research categorizes digital technology into four segments, such as the Internet of Things (IoT), robotics, mobile/social media and cognitive technologies which include artificial intelligence (AI) and big data analysis (BDA). It has been observed that when technologies are adopted combining these four categories, productivity increases. The market research data revealed that leaders have realized a higher overall return from robotics and mobile/social media. On the other side, followers have yielded benefits from cognitive technologies (Big Data Analysis and Artificial Intelligence) and IoT. It was also found that asset-heavy industries realized greater value from robotics and asset-light industries realized more value from mobile/social media. In a broader perspective, return on investment in digital technologies is overall positive. Though there is a trend of increasing operating costs due to potential investment in process adjustment, skill development and training, adoption of digital technologies leads to positive results in annual turnover. Hence, the initial dilemma regarding return on investment on digital technologies is no longer valid. Rather, companies that are avoiding digital technologies or moving forward with the wrong investment strategy will eventually be disrupted. So, it is essential to follow a structured strategy for investment in line with the company's business objective.

# 3

## Applicability of Digital Transformation

As per data analysis by a few global agencies, annual spending on the digital transformation between 2017 and 2020 increased from $0.96 trillion to $1.31 trillion. As per the various forecast, this spending is expected to reach $2.39 trillion in 2024. Investment in digital technologies is going to have a 53 per cent share of total global technology investment. The discrete and process manufacturing industry is going to spend about 30 per cent of the investment. Investment in Retail, Professional services and the transportation industry is also going to be significant. Various predictions say that financial services such as banking, insurance, security and investment services are going to see significant overall growth in digital investment. It is a known fact that digital transformation is having a huge impact on the IT and telecommunication industries. The forecasts show that globally all businesses across various industry sectors are providing importance to digital transformation spending (Figure 3.1). The nature and priority of investment vary depending on the industry sectors. There is no perfect method of classifying industry sectors. One of the globally recognized classifications is the Global Industry Classification Standard (GICS) developed by MSCI and Standard & Poor's (S&P) in the United States. As per GICS, there are 11 sectors as Energy, Materials, Industrials, Consumer Discretionary, Consumer Staples, Health Care, Financials, Information Technology, Telecommunication Services, Utilities and Real Estate. Each sector includes various industries. The industries under these sectors are adopting digital technologies. A few examples are provided in the following regarding digital technology adaption in different industries.

DOI: 10.4324/9781003270904-3

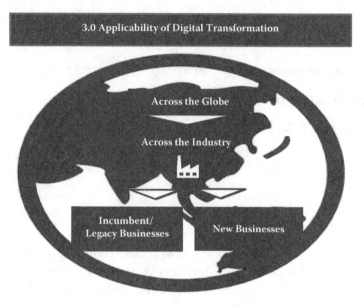

**FIGURE 3.1**
Applicability of Digital Transformation

For discrete and process manufacturing industries, the major spending priority is robotics, automation and root cause analysis. Also, manufacturing industries are gradually moving toward digitalizing the complete value chain, from product and process design to production and services. For example, one reputed industrial conglomerate has digitized its own electronics plant in Amberg, Germany with a 75 per cent automation rate. The output has been increased by a factor of 10 with a consistent number of employees. Only 11.5 defects occur per million products with a quality rate of 99.99885 per cent.

In the construction industry, there is a significant impact of digital technologies which include 3D scanning, Building Information Modelling (BIM) and the application of automated machinery and equipment. The application of digital technologies is a major feature for smart cities and smart homes.

The hotel industry, which is part of the Consumer Discretionary sector, is also gradually implementing digital transformation. For example, one reputed hotel chain adopted digital technologies to personalize customer experiences and prioritize customer relationships. In return, they have gained stronger customer loyalty by boosting revenue and market share. The retail industry's investment focus is on omni-channel commerce platforms and omnichannel order orchestration. Omnichannel retail integrates the different methods of shopping available to customers such as in a physical shop, online or by phone. The transport industry's priority is building energy management and freight management. For the food industry, there is significant scope for implementation of automation and digital transformation by improving the value chain and production system. By 2030, the implementation of IoT in the supply chain could reduce food loss by about 35 million tonnes. One of the interesting developments of collecting data and linking the same with a mathematical model of Insurance-Linked Credit is a significant development for the agricultural sector which is having an enormous social and financial impact.

## DIGITAL TRANSFORMATION IN STEEL AND METAL INDUSTRY

High-energy, material and asset-intensive complicated metallurgical processes such as steel production has always had a possibility for quality nonconformity. Recognizing the defect and tracing back the cause of the defect in operation and adjusting the processes according to the feedback to realize the "zero-defect" quality goal is one of the objectives of digital transformation in the steel and metal industry.

The two focus areas for any industry including steel and metal production are as follows:

- Maintaining quality for customer satisfaction
- Enhancing production

In the steel and metal industry, verticals for implementing digital technologies are Digital Data, Automation, Connectivity and Digital Customer Access (Figure 3.2).

### DIGITAL DATA

Capturing, processing and analyzing data with a feedback mechanism can empower a manufacturer to estimate process behavior and make a faster and smarter decision.

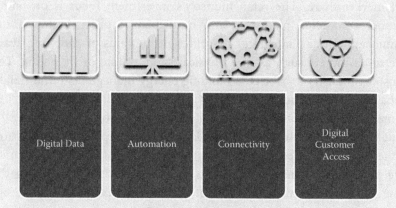

**FIGURE 3.2**
Digital Transformation Verticals in the Steel Industry

## AUTOMATION

Artificial Intelligence (AI), Machine Learning (ML) and Augmented Reality-based approaches can be implemented to automate production. These will reduce defects, increase operation speed and decrease operational costs.

## CONNECTIVITY

Interconnection of the complete value chain can improve communication, transparency and process efficiency.

## DIGITAL CUSTOMER ACCESS

By using a Digital Customer Access model, customers can directly connect with the business. This customer interface will improve transparency and direct feedback. It will also help in making an omnichannel service experience to suit changing customer behavior.

## WAY FORWARD

The steel and metal industry has already started adopting digital technologies to transform its business model. It is time for the steel industry to design and adapt a value-added digital strategy to expand the transformation experience.

**TABLE 3.1**

Identifying Industry Digital Initiatives

| | |
|---|---|
| Health | Virtual Care, Precision Medicine, Robotics, Intelligent Devices |
| Media | Over the Top (OTT), Content Communities, Crowdsource, Data Privacy and Transparency Reform, Phygital (Physical plus Digital), Advicetising (Advertising as Advice) |
| Electricity | Living Services, Real-Time Supply and Demand Platform, Energy Aggregation, Digital Customer Model |
| Logistics | Same-Day Delivery, Cross-Border Platforms, Shared Warehouse Capacity, Shared Transport Capacity, Circular Economy, Drones, Analytics as a Service |

A few examples of industry-specific digital initiatives are provided in Table 3.1.

These are limited examples of the vast application of digital transformation across industries. The examples in Table 3.1 are provided to showcase that industries in all sectors, across the globe, are implementing digital transformation to cope with the pace of the Industry 4.0 Revolution. To survive and succeed in a fast-moving market, an adaptation of digital technologies is becoming a mandatory requirement for all businesses.

Proper framework and application methodology along with cultural change is mandatory to realize the benefit of digital transformation.

## A SENIOR PROFESSIONAL'S VIEW: INTERVIEW WITH DR. DAVID G. HALLORAN, CHAIRMAN, HALLORAN ASSOCIATES, FLORIDA, USA

Dr. David G. Halloran graduated from Dartmouth College in 1953 in economics with winning senior thesis on the views of economist Dr. Maynard Keynes. Dr. Halloran was a US Navy fighter pilot from 1953 to 1961. After that, he was in the aerospace industry in business development jobs with business giants such as Douglas, which became McDonnell Douglas, the Martin Marietta in International sales of defence products to NATO and US Allies. Retired early in 1988, Dr. Halloran financed his own company Halloran Associates in Florida.

**What is the business profile of Halloran Associates?**

*Dr. Halloran*: Halloran Associates is a business data research-based consultant firm. It specializes in competitive pricing simulations of high-technology programs for clients in the field of aerospace and energy generations.

**How has digital influenced Halloran Associates?**

*Dr. Halloran*: We simply could not do all that we have done without digital. All communications are digital, some amplified by verbal, all research is done through the exploration of the vast digital information base available via the network and especially since the expansion to the cloud. The tracking capacity of digital once one gets into a subject matter is expansive. So much is recorded on the Net that one simply has to keep asking, asking, and asking and more data, some irrelevant, but much useful appears. Also, the profile we have built on competitors we are assessing for clients tends to accumulate digitally which gives the researcher the advantage of updates being sustained.

One word of caution, digital can also be used to provide false information just as readily as it can provide truthful information and the need to keep comparative files to cross-check is vital, and this is no different than the nondigital world where there is information, some very accurate, some partially so and some inaccurate to confuse the competition or wend off the market research community like us.

One thing we must remember is that digital is an enabler. However, one needs to have fundamental knowledge and core competencies to leverage a digital platform.

Regarding our model that effectively records all of our research is digital. We in Halloran Associates have applied our digital model to a variety of issues. Our team has come up with really credible resolutions.

**What about the digital skills of your team at Halloran Associates?**

*Dr. Halloran*: We started our company in the digital era. When we formed our group all were well acquainted with the technology, its advantages and its vulnerabilities. Today, job seekers in the technology industry have digital skills dating from high school forward. In today's world, it is essential for job seekers to acquire digital knowledge. Schools and universities should encourage students in this.

I was in the aerospace industry for 30 years. After retiring from Martin Marietta in 1988, I got finance for my company and also, I went back to college for my PhD at the University of Central Florida (UCF) to polish my math, computer science, and digital language and equation skills and became very close to Dr. Charles N. Millican, the founding president of UCF, who guided me on some special courses and skills that I passed on to my colleagues. School never stops particularly in the digital world which is in constant change via the addition of new approaches.

**How is digital going to affect the manufacturing sector globally?**

*Dr. Halloran*: That is a complex subject. My view is that when the process from research, to an idea, to postulation, to review of alternatives thereby defining competition, all these lead to not only a product but the most efficient way to design it, build it, ship it, support it and, very importantly, grow it so that it becomes the lead product or service in the market.

**How will technology advances impact the industry in the near future?**

*Dr. Halloran*: The key criteria are accuracy, content clarity and capacity, speed of transition, and multiplicity of transmission to multiple clouds and subclouds to sustain a competitive position. It is crucial to have an innovative and dynamic business framework.

# 4

## Digital Transformation Framework

How will a business embrace digital transformation? How will it formulate a digital transformation strategy? How will it invest in digital technologies? To answer these questions, businesses need to create a framework for digital transformation that includes strategy, enabler, process, governance and funding (Figure 4.1).

## 4.1 STRATEGY

Each business has a specific strategy. The strategy involves making choices that matter to businesses. The strategy is situational, dynamic and adapted to the needs of the enterprise. The main consideration of the strategy is to analyze the business environment and finalize the business objective and target.

Accordingly, finding the gap in existing capabilities and arranging facilities to bridge the gap is the focus of a strategy. That is how classically strategy works in a more predictable and nonmalleable market scenario. Predictability and malleability are two important factors for formulating a business strategy. Predictability is the degree that helps to forecast a business environment. Malleability refers to the degree which denotes alteration of the business environment by the actions of players in the market. Digital technologies are making the market highly unpredictable and malleable. By utilizing digital technologies, players in the market (either start-ups or incumbents) are trying to develop new concepts (processes/services/products) which have the potential to

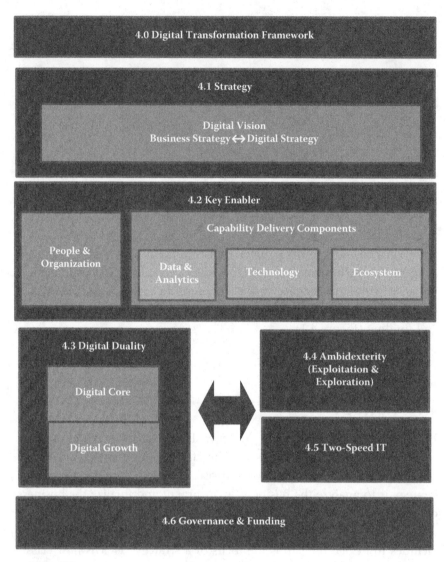

**FIGURE 4.1**
Framework for Digital Transformation

disrupt the existing business model and customer base. It applies to any sector and any industry. For example, in the steel industry, steel is no longer a mere product. Rather the concept of product service has evolved by applying the digital platform, which has the potential to reshape customer experiences. Therefore, steel businesses need to change their strategy from a conventional product sales model to a product-service offering model, which is the effect of digital technologies. The exponential growth of digital technologies is creating an enormous impact on business decision making. So, a business's overall strategy needs to focus on a digital platform. Instead of having a separate strategy for digital transformation, there is a need to bring digital thinking into an overall business strategy that will drive the entire business.

## WHAT IS DIGITAL THINKING?

Does digital thinking mean the implementation of digital technology to compete in the changing market?

The answer is no.

Digital thinking is much more than the implementation of digital technologies.

Elements of digital thinking are as follows.

### Speed

With the exponential growth of digital technologies, new processes and applications are evolving very fast, and it is impossible to know everything in this scenario. Even, while implementing any decision, it is not possible to know all its aspects. However, it is recommended to constantly evaluate whether enough information is available. If sufficient information is available, then implement the decision, without waiting for a full set of information. After implementation, collect feedback from important stakeholders and modify the action as soon as possible. Waiting for a full set of information is not recommended as it may cause a delay in implementation of the concept which may be detrimental for the business.

### Simplicity

Capability of the collective brains of the strategy team has limited power to process and analyze available data. Therefore, it is essential to keep the business objectives clear and concise. Research only be done on the essential things.

### Experimentation

The focus should be on experimentation, rather than planning. Full-fledged planning takes time and resources. But in the current volatile market, waiting for planning may be detrimental. Based on preliminary planning, experimentation of any newly conceived product/service/idea needs to be done. Based on the available information and feedback from the market, action should to be taken for modification.

### Collaboration

In this fast-changing scenario, every single business can't have its full-scale infrastructure. Businesses need to understand this limitation and outsource various activities to external stakeholders. A collaborative approach is needed with various other businesses that offer complementary facilities.

### Adaptability

The current business environment is fast changing. Businesses need to cope with the change and adapt to new concepts quickly.

Investment in digital transformation doesn't mean mere efficiency gain and customer intimacy enhancement by using advanced technologies. Rather the main factors are to create a digital vision and change people's mindset by reinventing organizational practices. Also, there is a need for a blueprinting arrangement of enablers to facilitate digital transformation.

### 4.1.1 Digital Vision

The business strategy must analyze the competitive environment and how it's likely to be affected. Fast-moving digital technologies are creating various opportunities for businesses and have tremendous potential to disrupt any sector. While finalizing strategy, all the possibilities and associated risks which can arise due to digital technology need to be assessed. For example, supply chain management for different companies is being reshaped due to Industry 4.0. Adopting technologies to continuously upgrade supply chain management is part of a strategic decision. So, the company leadership team has to align business strategy with digital needs. Accordingly, a digital strategy needs to be formulated that will enable the business to achieve its objectives. While choosing any digital application, the factors, such as the impact, competitive advantages and associated disadvantages for business, etc., need to be evaluated. A tire manufacturer's strategic decision to expand business opportunities by utilizing a digital platform is a typical example. By utilizing IoT-based technology, the company shifted the traditional business of selling tires to selling performance-centric outcomes which are backed by a money-back guarantee. In addition to developing a tire management system, they developed an ecosystem that includes telematics and training in eco-driving techniques. The service can effectively reduce fuel consumption by 2.5 litres per 100 kilometres drives, which has the potential to save $3,300 per annum for long-haul trucks (which is about a 2.1 per cent reduction in the total cost of ownership for truck fleet operators). It contributes to a reasonable reduction of carbon dioxide emissions as well.

## 4.2 KEY ENABLER

The framework must clearly define the enabling factors which drive the digital transformation process. The enabling factors are people, operating models, data and technology. Businesses need to cultivate a favorable culture by motivating people and building capabilities to deliver digital transformation processes.

### 4.2.1 People and Organization

Due to the advent of digital technologies, businesses have entered an age of continual innovation. Innovation is not limited to product or process only. Innovation in every level of business and organization is of paramount importance in today's industries. In today's fast-moving evolving market, the target is to maximize the value delivered to the customer or end user. Organizations need to improve efficiency by effective resource utilization, with the opportunity created by the digital platform. Adopting a digital platform is not about purchasing some software or digital service-oriented product and applying them in an organization that will start yielding profit beginning the next day. Rather there is a need for transformation in the overall approach of an organization, which hints at a change in the organizational culture. Culture is always driven by people. If the people do not have the right mindset to change and the organizational approach is not conducive to adopting a digital platform, the process of digital transformation will cause more trouble to the organization. To yield the maximum benefit of digital transformation, the business strategy has to focus on two important parameters: agility and way of work.

People are the most important factor in adapting agility and implementing a new way of work. The framework provides a guideline for upskilling employees in addition to utilizing their existing knowledge level. Also, the framework should provide an actionable guideline to facilitate change in mindset and organizational culture.

## AGILE

The traditional business model follows vertical integration, scale and standardization. It believes in planning and implementation of the plan to execute the market-ready final product or process or concept. However, as companies try to embrace the digital platform, the traditional model needs to be replaced with horizontal integration, agility and innovation.

Conceptually agile refers to an iterative approach for managing a project or developing software. As per the traditional approach, the final output is the focus which must comply with the specified requirements. However, in the agile approach, the team delivers the outcome even though it is not final, but in a consumable form. The requirement, result and customer reactions are monitored and evaluated continuously with a natural mechanism for quickly responding to change requirements. Agile approach functions based on feedback cycles and continuous improvement. The traditional approach is often known as a waterfall where one discipline performs its activities and delivers one level of output to the next discipline to carry out the next part of the activity. However, the agile approach performs with collaborative cross-functional teams. A few qualities of an agile approach are transparency, adaptation, inspection, feedback, collaboration and trust among stakeholders. Authentic human interactions are crucial where collaboration with the customer and communicative faster teamwork is important than rigid processes and predefined arrangements.

Companies can implement agility in four levels: team level, program level, portfolio level and enterprise organization level. Adaptation of organizational level agility is a complex and time-consuming process, which demands a holistic change in the existing operational model. Moving progressively from the team level to the organizational level can help businesses to change effectively. This complex large-scale process of achieving organizational agility is only possible when a business can inject a new way of thinking coupled with a new way of working.

## 4.2.2 Capability Delivery Components

Businesses need to create capabilities to adopt digital transformation. Data and analytics, technology, ecosystem and measuring indicators are capabilities that act as an enabler to implement and assess the digital transformation process.

### 4.2.2.1 Data and Analytics

Data is the core of digital transformation. An enormous amount of data used is generated from the day-to-day activities of the business. However, not many organizations capture and analyze these data effectively for value-added usage. Effective data management and analytics have the potential to become a competitive differentiator for a business. In a fast-moving digital economy, speed of decision making is crucial, where effective data and analytics competency plays a major role. Therefore, a business should consider data and analytics as a strategic priority.

The digital transformation framework should illustrate the authority of the person or persons that will be responsible for data management and analytics within the business. There should be a clear guideline for data identification, collection, quality, types of analysis and new practices.

The benefits of data and analytics have to be identified. Accordingly, across the business, the initiative needs to be taken so that the concept of data and analytics becomes an integral part of the business culture. The framework should provide a guideline for building or borrowing analytical competencies as part of business strategy.

The target is to create a data-driven business, which eventually has the potential to change the nature of work (related to data and analytics within the business) and the nature of the business, as a whole.

Also, a company has to plan and execute proper data policy in line with the company's business objectives and policies.

### 4.2.2.2 Technology

Technology and digital transformation have a symbiotic relationship. Technologies, such as cloud, IoT, Artificial Intelligence, Additive Manufacturing, etc., are real-time enablers or tools which need to be adapted to suit business requirements. Investment in digital technologies is significant. The digital transformation framework should provide high-level guidelines for the identification and selection of technologies to suit business requirements. Requirement and selection of digital technology should be an integral part of business strategy.

### 4.2.2.3 Ecosystem

Due to the extensive growth of Internet services and digital technologies, businesses are not only affected by their sectors, rather businesses can be affected by other players from different sectors. These are increasing the need for interrelation and interconnection of businesses, resulting creation of a business ecosystem. The business ecosystem comprises heterogeneous players in the market, such as suppliers, competitors, customers, etc., along with many multifaced relations. The concept of co-opetition is under the process of evolution where companies are building competitive capabilities through cooperation with other players in the market which includes competitors and customers. This is applicable for businesses whose core product is physical as well, such as manufacturing sectors. The framework for ecosystem economy has created an environment for worldwide interaction and amalgamation of different businesses by sharing resources and knowledge, crowdsourcing, and so on.

The process of building an ecosystem needs to be initiated to satisfy the customer's stated and unstated needs. To build an ecosystem, the digital transformation framework should focus on creating certain competencies and developing proper technological solutions as follows:

- Build flexibility in the company's operational system so that it can respond to changes and adapt.

- Create redundancy in the system so that a sufficient degree of certainty is built within the system with risk preparedness.
- Promote trust and mutuality.
- Endorse multiplicity in the domain of people, activities and ideas.

The framework should provide guidelines for the following:

- Identification of customers' requirements and value addition to enhance customers' experiences.
- Evaluation of business risks including risk forecast and opportunities.
- Identification of factors that are beyond control including external changes.
- Critical assessment of the company's capabilities and managing existing capabilities.
- Opportunities for cooperation with other companies and associated risks.
- Initiative of the people within the organization.

There should be clarity on the selection of ecosystem platform, considering features, offerings, flexibility, software and user-friendliness of the platform.

## 4.3 DIGITAL DUALITY

A company's digital transformation framework should focus on changing the existing legacy business into a more efficient organization by digitizing all business functions and, at the same time, promoting new innovative ideas for ensuring digital growth.

### 4.3.1 Digital Core

Customer expectations are changing with the advent of digital applications in various fields of life. The customer wants enhanced service from every transaction. This is irrespective of the type of transaction and type of purchase they are planning. For every transaction, the customer wants to interact more on the digital platform with a predictable experience, rather than physical interaction. To meet customer expectations, companies need to engage and deliver a persistent customer experience. Faster and simpler automated processes need to be designed to respond to evolving customer expectations. A seamless amalgamation of the entire value chain of the company's business is essential to deliver real-time information and services with predictable future actions. In this context data is the most essential part of the business. The existing running business model should be enhanced based on data that will seamlessly flow across the entire business operation. This is possible only when a company can focus on digitizing the whole business model by creating value from data at every level of business. Each function of the business has to be interactive with each other, based on the flow of data. The framework for digital transformation should guide the process of digitizing the core of the business.

## 4.3.2 Digital Growth

The purpose of digitizing all the functions (i.e. processes, internal and external transactions) is to make the running (legacy) business more data-driven and efficient. The company's existing IT department needs to attend to all the requirements so that the digitized process works smoothly for all functions. However, the company should be aware that, by utilizing the digital platforms (technologies and processes), numerous innovations are continuously evolving which can anytime create disruption, in some or other way. To safeguard the business, the company has to continuously explore options to develop a new product or service or business processes or functions. The company always needs to thrive to grow and change for the future. To ensure these growth options, the company can utilize fast-moving digital platforms in innovative ways. It can help the company to sustain even if disruption happens by other players in the market. Also, with the new growth options, the company can disrupt the market by creating new unexplored opportunities or the company can disrupt itself partially or fully before other players can disrupt it. To ensure digital growth, focused digital technology team(s) boosted with a new set of skills need to be identified and adopted. While preparing the company's digital framework, a high-level policy has to be framed to encourage agile digital thinking and to promote digital growth.

The digital transformation framework should explicitly mention an agile approach where failure is inevitable. The beauty of the approach is in its application modality. The requirement of application of the digital platform to encourage growth needs to be identified for a smaller section of a business function or a particular product or process. Hence, the scale of failure is limited to a small portion of the business without havoc financial or reputation risk. Due to its limited span of application, the failure is affordable and even convertible to new better alternative ideas. To reduce reputation risk, it is important to understand customer requirements by engaging customers in the development process. The development process starts with a keen understanding of the end-user's requirements, which helps to develop empathy with the end user. For any certain development process, follow the approach of design thinking using the steps of empathize, define, ideate, prototype and test (Figure 4.2). Once a failure is identified at any step, then it is important to go back to the earlier step suitably and make necessary changes.

Once the test is successful on a smaller scale, then the company can make a conscious decision to expand the new digital application in more departments or throughout the organization, based on the time, resource, risk and opportunity.

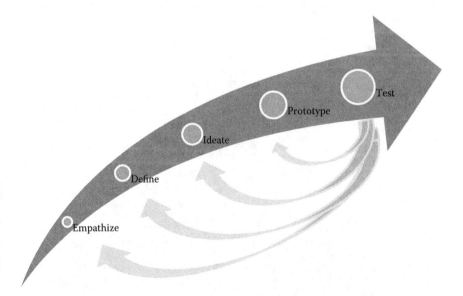

**FIGURE 4.2**
Steps for Digital Growth

## DIGITIZATION, DIGITALIZATION AND DIGITAL TRANSFORMATION

Digitization, digitalization and digital transformation are the most commonly used terms in modern business practices. How are they different from each other?

Digitization is shifting from an analogous form to digital form by changing physical attributes to digital objects. One example of digitization is scanning paper documents to be saved on a computer or entering data on a computer to save as digital files that were earlier done on paper. Digitization is one of the aspects to digitize the core.

Digitalization empowers business processes by using digitized data and digital technologies. An example of digitalization is uploading digital files to the cloud. It helps in utilizing data from multiple locations and using analytics to make appropriate business decisions. Digitization is one step for digitalization.

Digital transformation is the holistic change of business model with a broader vision and strategic objective. Digitalization of business processes is crucial for digital transformation (Figure 4.3).

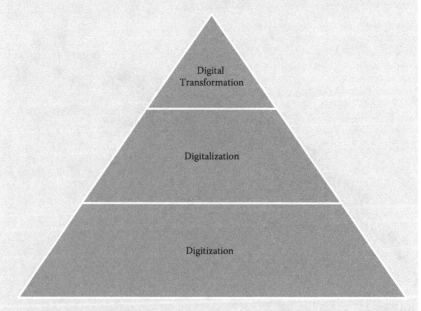

**FIGURE 4.3**
Digital Pyramid

## 4.4 AMBIDEXTERITY

As per Roman mythology, Jenus is the god of beginnings, transitions, time, duality and ending. He is portrayed as having two faces as he looks to the past and as well as to the future. Similarly, in today's challenging business environment, companies need to see backward constantly to attend to the existing processes, products and services, while looking forward to promoting innovation for future growth. This requires a strategic balance to exploit existing capabilities and explore new prospects. This phenomenon is called ambidexterity (Figure 4.4). This is not an easy job and very few companies have historically handled this duality efficiently. Ambidexterity enhances a company's performance. But at the same time, it causes tension between the two distinct capabilities which possesses a challenge for the company to create equilibrium between exploitation and exploration.

The strategy of prioritizing exploration over exploitation has the risk of suffering the cost of experimentation without gaining much of the benefit. The companies that focus on exploration exhibit multiple underdeveloped new ideas without considerable distinctive competencies. One of the telecom industry giants is a typical example. The company invested heavily in research and development through multiple technology centers and huge skilled manpower. At the peak, the company's R&D department had approximately 30,000 employees working at about 100 technology centers across the globe. However, despite focusing on exploration, the company's business performance declined considerably. As a result, the company laid off around 60,000 employees and closed the majority of its technology centers.

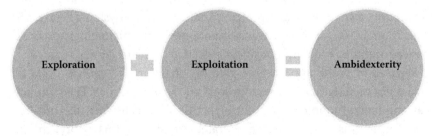

**FIGURE 4.4**
Components of Ambidexterity

Prioritized focus on exploitation is also risky. It makes the company feel safe as it promotes a comfort zone. In today's fast-moving innovative time, ignoring exploration can be dangerous for companies, as innovation will eventually arrive at the market which inevitably disrupts a company's business.

### 4.4.1 Why Is Ambidexterity Tough?

Exploitation and exploration are two different approaches, which require a different management style and mindset.

Exploitation is improvising existing processes and enhancing the existing model by improving efficiency. It typically facilitates short-term targets, centralization, discipline and standardization.

Exploration focuses on the long-term sustainability of a business. It requires flexibility and a decentralized structure. Exploration demands the concept of autonomy and risk appetite.

Ambidexterity is creating an equilibrium between two different aspects. Mature leadership is necessary to not only understand the theoretical requirement of ambidexterity that can rather strategize and implement both the contradictory aspects by introducing agility and a new way of working within the company.

### 4.4.2 How to Promote Ambidextrous Business?

Understanding the dynamic and diverse business environment is important for a company to create a balance between exploration and exploitation. Accordingly, the company needs to choose an appropriate approach for ambidexterity. Based on the dynamic business scenario, the company can become ambidextrous through four distinct approaches: separation, switching, self-organizing and external ecosystem (Figure 4.5). The framework for digital transformation should highlight approaches concerning the company's business objectives and strategy.

Separation is the approach of creating structurally separate units for two types of activities (i.e. explorations and exploitations). The company can implement ambidexterity through this approach when the business environment is diverse but moderately stable. In this approach, the company may adopt two different styles for matured or legacy business (which requires discipline and efficiency) and emerging business (for

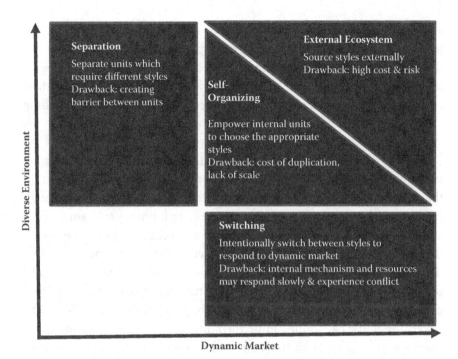

**FIGURE 4.5**
Strategy for Ambidexterity in Various Market Scenarios

which flexibility and innovation are key requirements). One example of separation is a global technology company's initiative to create an Emerging Business Organization (EBO) in 2000. EBO was formed to work separately from its existing business. The major component of EBO was quality leadership, tracking and monitoring, policy development, and sufficient resources. Between 2000 and 2005, the Emerging Business Organization added $15.2B to the main business. However, the approach separation has various drawbacks such as creating a barrier between units that prevent the flow of information and resources.

Switching is an approach where a company changes its style over time. In this approach, a company needs to adopt the exploratory style to innovate breakout product, service, technology or process. Over time, however, the company should switch to a more exploitative style for scaling up and securing a profitable market position. Switching is more appropriate when the market is dynamic but relatively less diverse. One American multinational technology company which focuses on e-commerce, digital streaming, cloud computing and artificial intelligence has utilized the switching concept effectively. Initially, it started the exploration of online retailing by use of the Internet. As it received a potential positive response from the market, it switched to exploitation by increasing the efficiency of the online retail business. In the switching approach, the company's internal mechanism and employees may respond slowly or experience conflict and resistance.

When a company deploys different styles concurrently, the managing switching process becomes intricate and infeasible for top management. In that environment, the self-organizing tactic is more apt for a company. In this approach, top management breaks the organization into small units and encourages each unit to adapt its style to meet the company's business objectives. This approach is appropriate when the environment is highly diverse, and the market is dynamic. One typical example of the self-organizing approach is a Chinese multinational home appliances and consumer electronics company which had created about 2,000 self-governing units. Each unit can perform independently such as an autonomous organization with its profit-and-loss statement, innovation program and operational methodology. It helped the company to survive bankruptcy in 1980 and become a market leader in the industry sector. In a self-organizing approach, a company may suffer considerable costs from duplication, and individual units may lack a business scale factor.

In a complex situation, when multiple strategic styles are needed and orchestrating the same by using internal resources is not possible, a company needs to adopt an external ecosystem approach. This approach is applicable in a highly dynamic market and diverse environment. An American multinational technology company that specializes in consumer electronics, software and online services has utilized the external ecosystem approach for the smartphone arena. By utilizing external agencies, the company have adopted different styles for different components of smartphones. As an example, content creation and corresponding app development require exploration due to changing customer needs and fast-moving competition. On the other hand, mobile component manufacturing and assembly are scale intensive and require a more classical exploitative approach. The external ecosystem approach is suitable in the most complex situation and it involves high costs and risks.

The framework for digital transformation should focus on strategic need and approach for ambidexterity. Ambidexterity is tough because it demands a constant change in styles and approaches. Most of the time, companies and their management are stuck under the success trap or perpetual search trap. Coming out of the prevailing trap and identifying a suitable approach for combined exploration and exploitation should be governed by the diversity and dynamics of the overall business environment. To achieve ambidexterity, when a company needs to digitize its core functions to increase internal efficiency by exploiting existing capabilities, it should grow by leveraging fast-moving digital technologies and platforms to explore new opportunities. The digital transformation framework provides a guideline for ambidexterity concerning the business environment and the company's overall business strategy.

## 4.5 TWO-SPEED IT

Every company has its existing legacy information technology (IT) architecture, which is built over a period of time to improve the efficiency of the legacy business. However, due to the rapid expansion of digital technologies, customer expectations are evolving very fast and every business (either the product or process or business value chain) is under the threat of disruption. To satisfy customers' changing requirements and to mitigate the risk of disruption, companies are transforming toward the digital business model, by adopting digital technologies and platforms. Companies need to strengthen their capabilities in various areas, such as digitizing core business processes and automating operation, innovating digital products and services, knowing customer behavior by using data and analytics and enhancing the multichannel experience for the customer (Figure 4.6).

Digitizing business processes (core) and automating operation is essential as it enables quick response times to customer, and helps in reducing operational costs by reducing waste and increasing efficiency.

Digital product innovation is important to address changing customer needs. One such example is linking a meteorological forecast with an agricultural loan by using a cloud server and analytics.

Understanding customer behavior by using data and analytics (with the consent of the customer) is significant business leverage for

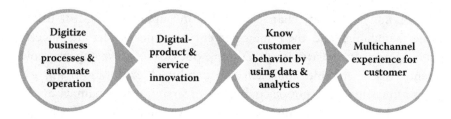

**FIGURE 4.6**
Four Major Vertical Digital Model Adaptations by Companies

companies to improve customer experience and to increase sales through effective cross-selling.

> ### CROSS-SELLING
>
> Cross-selling is the procedure of selling a different product or service to an existing customer. The cashier at the pizza store asks if the customer would like cheese toppings with the pizza is an example of cross-selling. Another example of cross-selling is when the online purchase website suggests an on-screen guard while a customer is buying a mobile handset.

Providing a seamless multichannel experience to the customer is effective in enhancing customer experiences. For example, many customers use online mobile apps to reserve a product and collect it from the nearest store.

Implementing the elements of four verticals poses a paramount challenge for the company's existing IT architecture. The legacy IT architecture, which helps in running the supply chain and operations systems responsible for accomplishing online product or service orders, lacks flexibility and rapidity. In today's competitive market, the company essentially needs to offer new products or services on a timely basis. The timely new offerings require periodic (maybe weekly or daily or some other interval) software releases for an online e-commerce platform. To achieve this type of speed, it is essential to have a software development approach with the inbuilt design thinking process. This approach is experimental. It runs with the concept of test-fail-learn-adapt-iterate. It allows an error in implementation and rectifies the error quickly based on working experience and live feedback. The legacy of IT architecture cannot allow this type of iterative approach. Because the quality of services in a legacy IT system is measured by the stability of the IT infrastructure, there is minimized risk in operation, compliance with regulatory norms, reduced number of errors of IT system, etc. On the other hand, an iterative IT system can manage errors in customer-facing areas or improvement areas where minor errors don't bring obligation, but which can enhance system efficiency and customer experience by the process of continual improvements. This iterative IT system needs to operate with higher speed compared to the legacy IT system. The digital transformation framework should provide an understanding of the scope, responsibility, implementation methodology and functionality of two-speed IT system. A two-speed IT system is important because it helps in improving the company's offerings and functional processes along with efficient robust core business operation by effective implementation of digitizing core and enhancing digital growth. Also, there should be a clear-cut technical understanding regarding integration between high-speed IT and legacy (traditional enterprise) IT system.

At the beginning of digital transformation adaptation, the company needs to implement the two-speed IT concept. However, as the digital transformation continues, based on the circumstances, the company may reduce the function of the traditional enterprise IT system and adopt a high-speed IT system throughout the organization. The existence of two-speed IT has a few drawbacks which can impact an organization, such as talent drain, hurry up and wait for, approach and realizing less benefit of the agile approach. The legacy IT system which runs with a waterfall approach works effectively when the target is fixed. But in today's market dynamics, fast change is predominant, where continuous adjustment is needed based on changing customer feedback, competitor's move and evolving regulatory norms. That is the reason being agile is essential. To move toward an all agile work environment, it is essential to gradually move toward a single-speed agile IT system.

## 4.6 GOVERNANCE AND FUNDING

The digital transformation framework should highlight governance structure and funding pattern for implementation of digital transformation. There can be a different approach to governance based on a company's business objectives. However, the creation of a governance committee is one of the best practices. The governance committee should include representatives from the digital team, which unites the business functions. The governance committee needs to be empowered to make decisions on whether to start or keep or kill projects. The governance committee needs to decide on fund initiatives as well and track the progress of agile fast-moving projects.

# 5

# *People and Organization Structure*

The preparation of digital transformation is not about making some trivial alterations to the existing rigid business processes. While start-ups are born with a digitally ready inbuilt agile work culture, the legacy businesses face genuine challenges such as lack of digital leadership skills, cultural stagnation, risk aversion and a long vertical chain of commands. For overcoming these challenges and adapting digital transformation, a profound cultural shift is essential. Participation of various stakeholders with early and frequent feedback is essential for bringing agile culture and a new way of work (WoW) (Figure 5.1).

## 5.1 AGILITY TRIO

Effective engagement, collaboration and equal sense of responsibility of people are essential for the successful implementation of an angile culture and the digital transformation process. This engagement is essentially the internal engagement of the company's leadership and employees. However, here the customer is also an important entity. The company should build open relationships with customers so they become interested in being a part of the company's agile way of work.

DOI: 10.4324/9781003270904-5

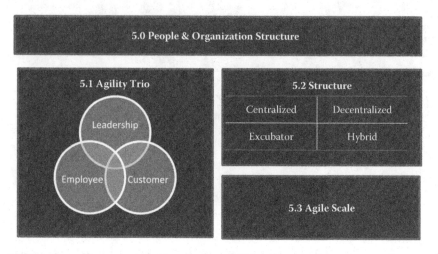

**FIGURE 5.1**
People Engagement in an Organizational Process

## 5.1.1 Leadership

A company's leadership should have a strong understanding of the necessities and prerequisites of the digital transformation process. The company's leadership should envisage a digital vision, create a culture of inclusiveness and effectively communicate with the entire organization by encouraging digital thinking and innovation. The leadership must understand that people are key in the process of digital transformation. Employees should be encouraged to think innovatively and communicate their pioneering ideas openly. Also, the company needs to identify the skill development requirements of its employees and further upskill or reskill them. Leadership should focus on a gradual shift toward the lean and liquid organization with a fewer chain of commands. Leadership should make a conscious decision to identify the steps for continuous improvement at a sustainable pace.

It's not only communication or forceful implementation of the new theoretical jargon-based digital transformation processes, but it is also more about sincere effort to encourage and engage employees to participate in the change to create an agile organization. More sincere the top

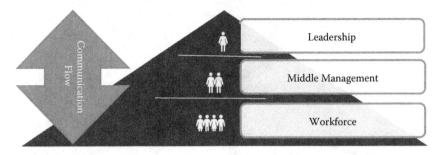

**FIGURE 5.2**
Organizational Leadership

management is to promote a genuine transparent leadership, easy for the organization to roll over agile culture across the organization. In this context, transformational leadership is more convincing to the employees to jointly participate in adopting a new way of work. Transformational leadership is about creating an open platform where top management and employees participate in the change processes and where employees have the right to an equivalent share of the company's resources with comparable opportunities driven by performance. In transformational leadership, leaders have the self-confidence to act in uncertain conditions but also have the humbleness to recognize what they don't know and honesty to being wrong. It's easy to say or preach, but tough to practice. It is real-time ego-less participation in organizational processes to empower subordinates to make an effective and efficient decision (Figure 5.2).

## TRANSFORMATIONAL LEADERSHIP

- Leaders inspire individuals, build trust and promote creativity and personal growth.
- Individuals develop a sense of purpose to help the group and organization. This goes beyond their self-interests, rewards or recognition for effort or devotion (Figure 5.3).

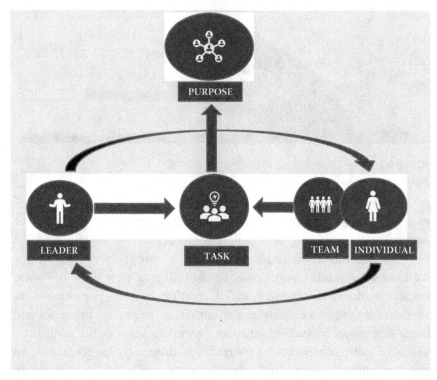

**FIGURE 5.3**
Transformational Leadership

## 5.1.2 Employees

Employee participation is an essential component for creating an agile organizational culture for a successful digital transformation. Agility is the value proposition of an employee's capacity to collect and disseminate information about environmental changes and respond to that information rapidly and pragmatically.

Employees need to be empowered to take faster action to solve problems. Employees should have productivity-enhancing technologies to take rapid action.

Employees need to have the freedom to experiment and learn from mistakes. The company may adopt tools such as risk management software to help team leaders understand the risk associated with experimentation. In the agile organization, employees mitigate the risk of experimentation by regularly sharing pertinent knowledge and proficiency across teams. The matrix structure of an organization may make it tough for employees to maintain clear expectations and lines of responsibility. So, in the case of matrix structure-based organizations, the company should initiate flexibility in interactions by creating a network of human beings.

### 5.1.3 Customers

The purpose of being agile is to serve the customer faster with value-added effective services. A customer-centric culture is core for an agile organization. Speed, adaptiveness and innovation are encouraged to serve needs and to improve the experience of the customer. An agile organization brings the customer in center stage by encouraging them to participate in the product development from inception.

## 5.2 STRUCTURE

Digital transformation calls for an organizational restructuring based on the way the company's strategy aims to embrace the digital application through an agile culture. To implement digitalization, the company can adopt any of the four organizational structure models, such as centralized, decentralized, excubator or hybrid (Figure 5.4).

In a decentralized approach, each business unit (BU) of the company is responsible for BU-specific digital initiatives. In this model, digital activities are embedded in each BU's strategy. This model is applicable when each BU has the capabilities to lead digital initiatives.

In the centralized model, a digital department led by Chief Digital Officer (CDO) is responsible for company-wide digital transformation. The centralized digital department needs to have a stronger connection with the leadership team. It helps the digital department to arrange resources and people that are required to generate competencies and mature scale. The digital department should work in close coordination with the individual BUs to support them to initiate digital activities. The digital department helps in creating a digital strategy that all the BUs follow.

Unlike the centralized or decentralized model, the excubator model of organization structure encourages the formation of a standalone unit to initiate digital activities. In this model, existing BUs are allowed to run on the legacy business model whereas the company creates a stand-alone

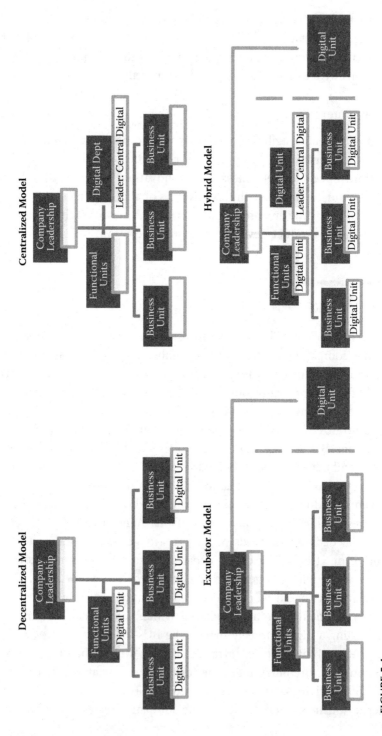

**FIGURE 5.4**

Organizational Structure

unit for digital applications and initiatives. The digital unit is created with a whole new set of capabilities and vision with its WoW for successfully starting the digital transformation process. To start the digital transformation process, excubator model can be effective as it has fewer chances of fiasco and thus the risk of failures is less.

As the company starts rolling the digital transformation processes, it can be effective if organizational structure shifts toward the hybrid model. This yields the benefit of all the models and reduces the risk of individual risks. In this model, the BUs implement digital initiatives and work to leverage the benefit of a centralized digital department led by a CDO. On the other hand, the company creates a parallel standalone unit that focuses on developing a new product or process which can provide a good competitive edge.

Digital initiatives are an ongoing process. Hence, a company's organizational structure, whichever is adopted to embrace digital transformation, needs to be flexible enough for adjustment to promote digital thinking and an agile WoW.

## 5.3 AGILE SCALE

Agile is an iterative approach that helps to deliver value to customers at a faster speed. To stay competitive in the market, companies need to transform themselves to become agile organizations.

A few of the features that an agile process can yield are as follows:

- Responding to customers' growing needs at a faster pace
- Providing flexible, tailored solutions
- Shifting the way of thinking to consider technology as part of a strategic enabler
- Delighting customers in the process

Not only should IT or software departments become agile, but other departments within a company should be encouraged to become agile. It helps to transform the organization and create a new way of thinking across the organization. The agile approach should be on an enterprise scale. Agile scale is a cultural change, where the people, processes and systems of the business must be involved in creating a value system by following an agile way of working.

What is the way to have a journey to scale agile?

For agile scaling, different businesses adopt different approaches or models. The agile scale emphasizes teamwork. Agile models suggest forming multiple teams within the organization that work based on their autonomous framework and people-centered culture.

Businesses can appreciate the merits and demerits of different methodologies and approaches. Accordingly, it can suitably adapt its way of working with the following essential features:

- Customer centricity for achieving organizational growth
- Defined structural changes within the organization
- Agile practices and pace
- Matured approach to accept changes
- Managing and improving agile team dependencies
- Lean approach and design thinking
- Bottom-up and top-down approach

For scaling agile, companies need to sustainably change their organizational way of working. This is not an overnight process; it must be sustained and aligned with the company's strategy. Therefore, the company needs to find appropriate resources. If needed, the company hires new employees that are familiar with an agile way of working. Existing employees with legacy technology knowledge and new agile employees will create a perfect multidisciplinary mix.

### AGILE IS ABOUT VALUE DELIVERY

Samik Mukherjee has been working in the IT sector since 2000. He has experienced the different phases of transformation of the IT industry in India and other countries. He began his agile journey in 2017 and has been a part of several transformation initiatives since then. He is an enthusiastic *Agilist* by passion and profession.

Samik has spoken about agile and shared his experience in an interview.

**It is said that Agile is based on Empiricism. What does this mean?**

*Mukherjee:* Empiricism is a process based on experience. Whatever we experience, based on that we modify our reaction, behavior, process or effort.

Empiricism is based on trust. Transparency, inspection and adaptation are key elements of Empiricism.

In a complex environment, we regularly inspect and adapt to navigate through our way. That is basic human nature, which is reflected in every aspect of our lives. We just keep it transparent while inspecting and adapting which helps us to progress in life. Inspect and adapt is nothing but collecting feedback on progress so far and based on the feedback take decision on the next level of progress.

Trust is also necessary to keep us progressing. In the entire process of the journey, be it in our professional world, be it in the personal sphere, if trust is lost, everything is lost. Having a mutual sense of trust is necessary among stakeholders in a journey.

Agile works in a complex environment where most of the future is unknown. Empiricism helps in such a situation. Delivering early and often, receiving early and frequent feedback based on delivery, and continuously improving the development journey based on the feedback loop is the core essence of Agility.

**How does Agile leadership differ from traditional leadership? How does leadership interact with employees in an Agile culture?**

*Mukherjee:* Traditional leadership is vertical. Information flows from the top down. Ideas are made, visions are created, and the path is planned at the top, and then they flow down the ladder as orders. In traditional leadership, it is expected that those in the lower level should follow the orders instead of challenging them. Traditional leadership believes in command and control and trusts less to its employees. Traditional leadership relies more on established processes than human emotions and interactions.

Agile leadership, on the other hand, is more human-centric. It does not command and control, rather it enables the employees to become more self-managing, self-organizing. Agile leadership is horizontal leadership. In agile leadership, designations are not to show power but to show the collaboration within the organization for proper functioning and adding value to its customers. Agile leaders do not decree orders. They enable people so that the work is done. Agile leaders decentralize most of the decision-making systems.

A traditional leader says, "I want this task to be finished by Friday." The agile leader says, "How can I help you so that you can deliver this task by Friday?"

**What role does the customer play in an Agile transformation?**

*Mukherjee:* Customers will only show interest in your company's agile transformation if they see value for them in it. It is, therefore, really important for both an organization and its customers to know and agree on what defines value for them.

Being an employee of a service-driven organization for quite a long time, I have seen transformations to be initiated or envisioned. When we talk about transformation, only getting the organization transformed through its employees is not sufficient. To achieve and sustain Agility, it is also important that the employees and leadership maintain an Agile environment and follow a new way of work.

Customers are very much part of that way of work because an organization survives and excels only by serving its customers better. So, it is important to onboard customers in an organization's journey toward Agility. I have seen this handholding happening in multiple ways. Sometimes, the customer was more advanced in the Agile way of working, it mandated and helped the service organization to become matured in Agile way of working, to continue the journey together. In other cases, I have seen the service organization itself holding the hand of the customer organization, explaining to them the value addition by embracing Agility, and helping them to become Agile matured.

In this way of work, the customer understands how planning is made, how to set expectations and how to synchronize to the main mantra of Agility – deliver value early and often, gather feedback early and frequently. They then effectively become part of Empirical practice, which helps both the service organization (by being able to deliver value more frequently) and the customer organization (by getting the value delivered early and often).

**Is Agile better than the traditional way of working?**

*Mukherjee:* Agile is different from the traditional way of working. It has a different approach. It gives priority to outcome over output. It works in the human sense. It focuses on value delivery, early and often. These are the new offerings from Agile which were not present in earlier "traditional" ways of working. Now if in your organization, these offerings from the Agile way of working bring more value than the traditional way of working, then it is better for you to adapt to Agile.

Agile does not look lucrative to every industry. Think of the pharmaceutical industry. They research and manufacture drugs. To bring a drug to the market, they have to spend big effort on research and analysis. To launch a drug in the market there is a need for years of R&D effort. So, time-to-market, or early value delivery is never a priority for the pharma industry. They cannot run in a competition for launching a life-saver drug. Their motto is saving lives, they have to take utmost precaution before launching a drug. Agile, on large scale, does not work effectively in such a scenario. Of course, to expedite internal processes Pharma companies can adapt to the Agile way of working, but Agility simply does not work on their ultimate value delivery. A traditional, phase-based approach (in form of clinical trials, etc.) suits better in this type of industry.

**Agile techniques have become one of the fastest-growing and most popular aspects of the IT industry. Can Agile be used for non-software projects?**

*Mukherjee:* The Agile concept started in the 1990s and the beginning of the twenty-first century. It began as a response to the growing needs of the software development and IT industry.

IT was a separate, specialized industry by then, 20 years ago from now. The world has changed a lot in the past 20 years. Today IT is part of almost every industry, be it the core engineering or medicine or commerce or the entertainment industry. For example, in 2001, I used to take time from my schedule to stand in a queue to pay my electric bill, today I can pay it from my smartphone.

Agile is about value delivery. Early and often. If any business finds this as crucial to support survival, it embraces the Agile way of work.

I, personally, am a part of few Agile teams for a Dutch manufacturing company. None of my team deals with any software or IT per se. All my team members come from different departments that deal with laptop/desktop allocation, floor management, auditorium management, audio-video-telephony equipment management, lighting and noise-cancellation arrangements for meeting rooms, etc. We are Agile. We do incremental value delivery.

**What is scaling Agile? Is it different from Agile?**

*Mukherjee:* Scaling Agile is not different from Agile. Scaling is a process of extending Agility in an organization. If you consider an Agile team like a family, then scaled Agile is like a family of families.

The essence of Agile remains the same. We deliver value, early and often. When we talk about Agile teams, the team collaborates with its members and produces value. But an organization cannot be run by just a few Agile teams working on their own. There are interactions, dependencies, agreements that often happen across teams. When an organization, consisting of multiple agile teams work in synchronization, collaborates as and when needed and deliver value to its customers, stakeholders or end users, then we say that the organization is scaling up in Agility.

There are multiple scaling frameworks available in practice.

A full-scale transformation takes a long time for a standard organization, and even after that, it doesn't reach any destination. Scaling Agile transformation is an ongoing journey, and it happens through multiple waves.

I have been part of scaling transformation partly with one of my customers. You cannot just start practicing scaling Agile suddenly. Agile is more about mindset, behavioral change. Introducing scaling in a big bang approach never works out, also scaling needs a certain level of maturity at the organization level. It is, therefore, always good to start with small teams, practice Agile at the team level for a few years, and then start with mini-scaling frameworks. If the mini scaling becomes effective, organizations can think of the next level of scaling such as forming programs and value streams. That goes for the next few years.

It's a long-term approach, there is no fixed timeline in achieving scaling, it varies depending on geographical location, nature of business, organizational culture and many other factors. In short, Agility cannot be planned, neither can be predicted. While introducing scaling transformation to an organization, this has to be remembered.

**Can scaling Agile fail?**

*Mukherjee:* Scaling Agile can fail. Forget about scaling, even initial adaptation of Agile also fails. And there can be multiple reasons for failure.

Practicing scaling requires a certain level of maturity in basic Agile. If an organization starts scaling without attaining the basic level of Agility, it can fail. And when I say it "can" fail, I mean to say it can still be successful too. It all depends on how the organization learns from its failure, how soon it can inspect and adapt. If the organization culture is responsive enough to recalibrate its journey, it can still be successful at a certain level.

Other reasons may include stressing too much on processes and tools than transforming mindsets, behaviors and cultures; planning achievement timeline for scaling Agility in a traditional method; identifying potential scapegoats for intermediate failures and punishing them; failing to nurture and maintain a fail-safe, trustworthy environment and psychological safety, and so on.

**What is the future of Agile?**

*Mukherjee:* Agile works on core human sense with human values. Agility is a process to transform our operations from being reliable on processes to being reliable on human instincts. I don't see any reason to deviate from core human-centric approaches in the future.

If in case, we start seeing less value addition through Agile methodologies and we invent another process in the future, that also will happen through inspection and adaptation. You cannot really avoid Agile in your life.

# 6

## *Capability Delivery Activities*

Capability delivery represents processes and enablers that need to be demonstrated to implement digital transformation in an organization. The capability delivery activities need to be carried out to ensure a balance between cost of the adopted digital transformation process and performance to mitigate an agreed level of risk. Performance is typically referred to as a quantifiable measurement of the digital transformation process such as speed of new technology implementation, response time to resolve issues/outages, number of new customers/segments/sectors from new products and services, customer reviews and feedback, employee engagement score, etc., for an agreed time frame, over which risks need to be identified and mitigated through an agile way of work. Risk, performance and cost are the buzzwords that need to be sensibly addressed throughout the agile journey of the product, process and organization. Capability delivery activities are broadly categorized into two parts, such as process deliveries and enablers required for digital transformation (Figure 6.1).

## 6.1 PROCESS DELIVERY

In addition to creating an agile work culture, as per the digital transformation framework, a company needs to take action related to two important process implementations: digitize the core and digital growth.

DOI: 10.4324/9781003270904-6

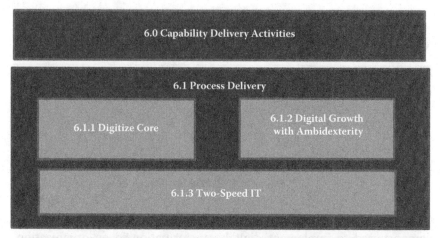

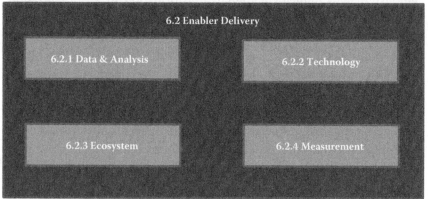

**FIGURE 6.1**
Capability Delivery Activities

## 6.1.1 *Digitize Core*

Three steps that can be useful for digitizing the core are process mapping of the business functions by creating a process flow diagram, automating the processes identified in the flow diagram and continuously updating the automated processes (Figure 6.2).

### 6.1.1.1 *Process Flow Diagram Creation*

The first step in digitizing the entire workflow is to understand the company's existing processes and thereafter prepare a process workflow diagram for process mapping. This is a visual representation of how

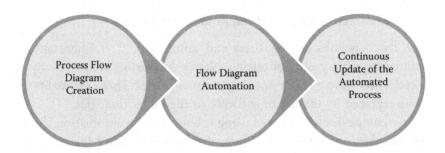

**FIGURE 6.2**
Steps to Digitize the Core

different functions or departments work for their various deliverables and how they interact with each other.

For process flow diagram creation, discussions are required across various departments and a true picture of the existing workflow should be developed. Process mapping also needs to be carried out for support functions such as Human Resources, Administration, Accounts, etc. Process workflow diagrams help everyone in the company understand who performs what work and in which order. The workflow diagram must capture the true representation of the existing way of work within the company.

After preparation of the workflow diagram, it is necessary to identify inefficiencies and waste in the existing process. Accordingly, the effort is to improve the existing workflow by removing waste. The target is to create a lean workflow structure where steps can be digitized.

### 6.1.1.2 Flow Diagram Automation

After finalizing the workflow diagram, the next step is to automate the processes. By using software, the workflow can be digitized. To digitize, it is necessary to create a provision of data input in software at each stage which will eventually generate output data. It is essential to use that output data as input for the next activity in the flow diagram.

In the automated process, a person in the workflow chain is required to enter the necessary information into the software. There should be a provision in the software to attach soft files. Then, automatically, the job is designed to reach the next person in the chain. So, through the software, the tasks are automatically assigned to the concerned person by creating a clear data trail.

### 6.1.1.3 Continuous Update of the Automated Process

Once the processes are digitized and automated, it is important to continue improving and optimizing. As per the existing system, many of the tasks may have a requirement of manual entries. Those manual tasks can be replaced by the use of software or digital technologies.

Many companies have started using robotic process automation (RPA) to reduce human interface and to replace human worker for repetitive tasks which helps in accelerating the process and reducing human errors.

Digitizing the core business processes is an incremental, ongoing process. It involves utilizing different technologies for various steps of digitization. It is important to use a new technology platform and software which can be seamlessly integrated with the existing IT environment of the company.

## 6.1.2 *Digital Growth with Ambidexterity*

Pursuing digital growth by focusing on new opportunities cannot be the company's only objective, as it has to maintain and improve the existing business. When a company plans to explore digital growth, ambidexterity needs to be obtained. The mantra is to become ambidextrous by exploiting the core business and exploring new opportunities. The company should understand the level of diverse environments and dynamic market scenarios. Accordingly, based on the digital transformation framework, the company has to plan the implementation strategy. These strategies are separation, switching, self-organizing or external ecosystem. These strategies are overall modalities to become ambidextrous, where innovation by exploring digital growth is the key.

For exploration, the company needs to plan innovation with different dimensions, such as incremental innovation, sustaining innovation, disruptive innovation and radical innovation. The company has to explore all the innovation styles by forming an innovation matrix. This prepares the company for the probable changes in a dynamic market scenario (Figure 6.3).

The company should prepare an Innovation Chart (Figure 6.4). The chart needs to be filled in and periodically reviewed for different sets of customers. This will help the company understand the innovation initiatives in various categories. Accordingly, the company can explore

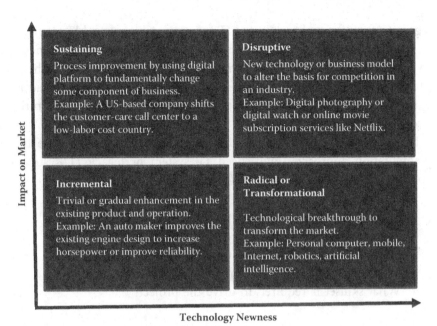

**FIGURE 6.3**
Innovation Matrix

| Type of Innovation | Incremental | Sustaining | Discontinuous | Radical |
|---|---|---|---|---|
| **New Customers** | | | | |
| | | | | |
| | | | | |
| **Existing Customers** | | | | |
| | | | | |
| | | | | |

**FIGURE 6.4**
Innovation Chart

different types of innovations. In the case of a new resource requirement, a decision can be made to initiate necessary action.

## 6.1.3 *Two-Speed IT*

In today's market, customers expect fast and innovative solutions. To have a balance between stability and speed, organizations need both the legacy IT function and high-speed IT function. A high-speed IT team can be employed for new developments (for product or process) which needs to be implemented through fast-track project management. Whether a project has to be executed by legacy IT functions or by a high-speed IT team, the company has to assess the requirement through a structured needs and demand analysis.

For a particular requirement, the company has to evaluate the implementation approach (high-speed IT system or legacy IT systems) concerning the following criteria (Figure 6.5):

- What is the objective of the project?
- What is the technological need for the project?
- What is the time frame for implementation?
- What approach is needed for implementation?
- What skillset is required to drive the project?

If the objective of an IT project is to increase the efficiency of the organization then implementation through a legacy IT system is the best approach that uses enterprise architecture defined technologies. However, a high-speed IT system is more appropriate when the organization wants to build product leadership or enhance customer familiarity with the help of emerging technologies.

High-speed IT implementation focuses on digital thinking to develop a minimum viable product. The minimum viable product has limited functionality, support capability and scalability. A minimum viable product can be matured into an enterprise application within the framework of the legacy IT system. Hence, it is essential to integrate both the IT system.

Important factors for seamless integration between high-speed IT and legacy IT are as follows:

- High-speed IT should follow the common architecture and design principles of a legacy IT system.
- High-speed IT should follow common coding standards of a legacy IT system so that code of the minimum viable product can be used while developing an enterprise solution.

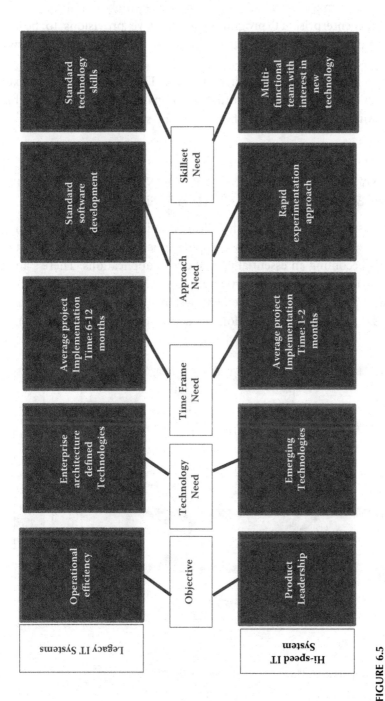

**FIGURE 6.5**
Criteria for Selection of IT System

- The minimum viable product should be entirely reusable.
- Large enterprise IT programs should have provisions to be decomposed into logical parts so that these can be explored by using high-speed IT if required.
- The legacy IT system and high-speed IT system should co-exist with defined objectives until the company's digital platform has matured to follow only a high-speed IT system.

## HOW CAN SEAMLESS INTEGRATION BETWEEN HIGH-SPEED IT AND A LEGACY IT SYSTEM BE ACHIEVED?

The answer is API (Application Programming Interface). API is a software agent that allows two applications to talk to each other. API is becoming an essential part of digital applications. There's an API at the back end of every application that links and supports digital interactions in engagement systems. APIs are used on the backside for linking applications to data and services (Figure 6.6).

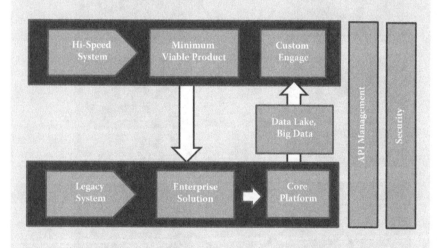

**FIGURE 6.6**
Integration between High-zspeed IT and Legacy IT

## 6.2 ENABLER DELIVERY

The company needs to select appropriate enablers which essentially help to develop capabilities to deliver the digital transformation process. In the agile organization, major enablers are Data and Analytics, Technology and A Business Ecosystem.

### 6.2.1 *Data and Analytics*

The whole digital transformation process evolves around data: data collection, processing, storage, utilization and communication. The company needs to develop capabilities for Data and Analytics. The first step for building Data and Analytics competencies is to have a clear vision. The company's management and the digital transformation leaders need to find out the purpose and way forward for building up Data and Analytics capabilities.

> ### DATA ANALYSIS AND DATA ANALYTICS
>
> Data Analytics is a broader term. Data Analysis is part of data analytics. Data Analytics consist of data collection, organization, processing, analysis, storage and the tools and techniques used to handle data.

The company has to think about how to effectively use data and analytics for improving its process and product. The next steps are to find out tools to effectively use data and analytics.

Following are a few action areas for enhancing data and analytics capabilities:

- Modernize a legacy IT system such as ERP and mainframe. API and microservices increase the modularity of applications across the organization.
- Company needs to create a data lake to effectively use data.
- Cloud migration to deliver universal data access.

## DATA POLICY

Doing business without a defined data policy is one of the riskiest tasks for a business. The major reasons for data policy are fulfilling legal requirements and enhancing customer confidence. Data policy describes how a company must collect, track and store data, especially customer data.

While forming a data policy, the company should consider the following:

- Ownership of the data
- Type of data to be used for business benefit
- Type of data to be shared
- Any external agency or entity to whom data may be or need to be shared

Depending on the business objective and policy, a company needs to address the above considerations.

What needs to be considered in data policy?

- Understand the law of land

The company must recognize that customers have a legal right to know about how the company uses their data. To protect the customer's legal rights, the company needs to know local laws relating to data privacy. If required, the company should consult a lawyer. If the business is spread among multiple countries, then the company needs to understand the data privacy laws of those countries as well.

- Follow changes in the law

Due to various controversies, every country used to revisit the data privacy law as and when required. The company needs to assign someone to follow the latest developments of data privacy issues and changes in the law, so that the company's data policy can be updated suitably.

- Be ethical

If the company thinks that they can do anything with customers' data by complying with the law, then it is not always right. The company needs to think about whether the data policy is ethical or not. If customers lose confidence in the company and become suspicious about the company's activities with personal data, that may have a detrimental effect on the future business.

Data policy is one of the vital aspects of the business but often neglected. The company needs to consider data policy with utter seriousness.

A company has to consider internal data handling by its employees and partners as well. The company should adopt a user-friendly centralized platform where everyone across the company uses the same data without any probability of distortion. The company needs to support employees for having an effective net connection for accessing data at the right time for the right purpose.

## 6.2.2 Technology

Proper selection of technologies for business purposes is crucial. A few of the important and popular digital technologies which are used by modern businesses extensively are Big Data, Cloud, Internet of Things, Cybersecurity, Additive Manufacturing, Artificial Intelligence, Machine Learning and Blockchain (Figure 6.7).

### 6.2.2.1 Big Data

Big Data is a large and complex set of data. These voluminous data set can be used for business purposes if they are stored, processed and communicated effectively and efficiently. However, due to the enormous volume, conventional data processing software cannot handle them purposefully.

The concept of big data become popular in the first decade of the twenty-first century. An open-source framework, such as Hadoop and

**FIGURE 6.7**
Digital Technologies

Spark, becomes instrumental in storing, processing, analyzing and communicating big data faster and cheaper.

The concept of big data is based on five Vs: Volume, Velocity, Variety, Value and Veracity.

## Volume

In today's time, a massive volume of unstructured data generates through various sources. Proper collection, storage, process, analyze and communication of these data are hitherto impossible by conventional software. With the advent of digital platforms, it becomes possible to handle these big data sets.

## Velocity

Data generation and collection rates have become faster. Collection of data and analysis faster for quick and timely business use is a real success of digital platforms.

## Variety

When a massive data set is generated from multiple sources and multiple modes, naturally they are not fully structured. Digital technologies made the data possible to process with a fit for purpose.

## Value

Thanks to digital technologies, big data becomes capital as data possesses intrinsic values.

## Veracity

Due to modern digital technologies, data handling costs have reduced considerably. Big data is now cheaper and more accessible. It has helped in making accurate and precise business decisions.

Big data is used for various business purposes, such as predictive maintenance, machine learning, fraud and compliance, operational efficiency, innovation, customer experiences and product development.

Companies should follow certain best practices while investing in big data:

- Aligning unstructured with structured data.
- Aligning big data with specific business goals.
- Overcoming skill shortage with standards and governance.
- Optimizing knowledge transfer.
- Planning discovery lab to ensure high-performance work area.

Big data technology is evolving at a fast pace. Apache Hadoop was the commonly used technology to handle big data initially. Then Apache Spark arrived in 2014, followed by a combination of the two frameworks.

### 6.2.2.2 Cloud

The "cloud" denotes servers that are accessible over the Internet. It includes databases and software that run on those servers. Cloud servers are situated in data centers all over the world.

Cloud computing refers to the delivery of computing services over the Internet. The services include servers, storage, networking, databases, analytics, software and intelligence.

The major advantages of the Cloud are cost, flexibility, global scale, productivity, performance, reliability and security.

**Cost**

Cloud computing removes capital expenditure for the purchase of hardware and software and setup, electricity for power and cooling, the racks of servers, and the IT experts to maintain the infrastructure.

**Flexibility**

Cloud allows businesses to be more flexible in work practices. Cloud services can be accessed from any locations, with the help of Internet connections. It provides faster services that can be accomplished with few mouse clicks.

**Global Scale**

Cloud services provide the ability to scale. Cloud provides the right scale of computing power, storage and bandwidth from any location.

**Productivity**

IT teams need not focus on maintaining their servers. It reduces the workload of IT personnel so they can concentrate on other important work.

**Performance**

The cloud services run on a worldwide network of protected data centers, which are updated regularly to the latest, fast and most efficient computing hardware.

**Reliability**

Cloud makes data backup, disaster retrieval and service continuity easier and less expensive.

**Security**

Cloud providers offer policies, technologies and controls that enhance security.

The types of cloud services include SaaS, PaaS, IaaS and serverless.

### 6.2.2.2.1 Software as a Service (SaaS)

Software as a Service is a technique for delivering software applications over the Internet. With software as a Service, cloud providers host and maintain the software application and underlying infrastructure. Users connect to the application, usually with a web browser on their phone, tablet or PC, by using the Internet.

### 6.2.2.2.2 Platform as a Service (PaaS)

Platform as a Service refers to cloud services for developing, testing, transporting and maintaining software applications. By using PaaS, developers can quickly create web or mobile apps.

### 6.2.2.2.3 Infrastructure as a Service (IaaS)

Infrastructure as a Service is the fundamental category of cloud services, where IT infrastructure can be rented. The infrastructure refers to servers, virtual machines (VMs), networks, storage, operating systems.

*6.2.2.2.4 Serverless Computing*

In the Serverless computing model, cloud providers allocate on-demand machine resources by taking care of the servers on behalf of their customers. In this execution model customers are charged based on usage, but not for a fixed amount of bandwidth or number of servers.

### 6.2.2.3 Internet of Things

Internet of Things (IoT) refers to the network of objects (described as "Things") that communicate with each other over the Internet. Things can be anything and everything. Sensors, software and other digital technologies are attached to the things which help communicate between each other. It is not only computers or mobile, IoT can connect all the things of the world and make them talk to each other.

In IoT, essential components can be divided into three categories:

- *Sensors that collect and send information*: Sensors, which could be a light sensor, temperature sensor, air quality sensor, material sensor or any other sensor with a purpose, automatically collect information from the intended environment and transfer the same to the target component with the help of defined connections.
- *Components that receive and act on information*: There are components or machines which receive information and act upon it in a defined way. Examples include computer printers or cars.
- *Components that do both*: The most interesting part of IoT includes the components that not only collect information and send but also receive information and act on it. Collected information is sent to supercomputers which make sense of all the information.

IoT has extended the power of the Internet beyond computers and smartphones to a whole span of things and processes.

By using low-cost computing, big data, the cloud and mobile technologies, physical things can collect, analyze and share data with minimal interference. It is a connection between the physical world and the digital world.

IoT helps companies in many ways such as:

- To derive data-driven insight which is helpful in business decision making.

- To increase productivity and efficiency of business operations.
- To connect the physical world with the digital world which is helpful in value creation.

## NETWORK GENERATION

Improvement in network generation has a significant impact on innovation across many industries. It is creating opportunities for emerging technologies such as the IoT to become ingrained in our economy and way of life. Various network generations such as 1G, 2G, 3G, 4G and 5G are gradually improving communication efficiency.

Mobile phone companies started deploying the fifth-generation wireless mobile network (5G) in 2019. 5G is about voice and texting along with data at the fastest ever speed. 5G enables the creation of a new type of network that connects practically everyone and everything that includes multiple objects, machines and gadgets.

One of the significant features of improved network generation is reduced latency. In a network, latency refers to the time it takes to capture, transmit, process through various gadgets and decode a set of data at the target point. Reduced latency of the improved network generation is improving responsiveness and accuracy.

In addition to mass-scale IoT applications, improved network generation is opening opportunities for enhanced mobile broadband, remote-controlled critical infrastructure and artificial intelligence. Further improvement of network generation will have a far-reaching impact on human civilization.

### 6.2.2.4 Cybersecurity

The biggest challenge in today's digital world are cyberthreats. Cyberattack numbers are increasing rapidly. Medical services, retailers, financial services and public entities experience most breaches where malicious criminals are responsible for the majority of the cases.

There can be three categories of cyberthreats as follows:

- *Cybercrime*: Cybercrime is a case where individuals or groups target systems for financial gain or to cause disruption.

- *Cyberattacks*: Cyberattacks generally happen to gather politically motivated information.
- *Cyberterrorism*: Cyberterrorism intends to create panic and fear.

As cyberthreats are rising rapidly with malicious attacks, companies are increasing their cybersecurity budget.

### 6.2.2.4.1 How Do Cyberthreats Happen?

Malware, phishing, SQL injections, man-in-the-middle and denial-of-service attacks are a few cybersecurity threats.

- Malware
  Malware (malicious software) is sent to target people or organizations through an unsolicited email attachment or legitimate-looking download. Malicious software is a common cyberthreat that attempts to damage or disrupt a computer or system. Cybercriminals use malware for monetary fraud or politically motivated cyberattacks.

  A few examples of malware are:
  - *Virus*: A virus is a self-replicating program that attacks and spreads across a computer system by infecting files through malicious code.
  - *Spyware*: Spyware is a software program that cybercriminals use to send and secretly record user activities and information.
  - *Ransomware*: Ransomware is sent by cybercriminals to lock down user files with the threat of erasing data unless a ransom is paid.
  - *Trojans*: Trojans are legitimate-looking software sent by cyber-criminals to damage a computer system.
  - *Adware*: Adware is an advertising software used as malware.

- Phishing
  Phishing is an approach to send emails from a legitimate-looking company, asking for sensitive information.

- SQL Injection
  SQL (structured query language) injection is used by cybercriminals to take control and steal data from data-driven applications.

- Man-in-the-middle attacks
  In an unsecured WiFi network, the cybercriminals can track data being passed from the user's device to the network. This type of cyberthreat is called a man-in-the-middle attack.

- Denial-of-service attacks
  A denial-of-service attack is an approach where network and servers are jammed with traffic so that the victim's computer system cannot perform legitimate activities.

To avoid these cyberthreats, it is essential to have proper cybersecurity. The following are the categories of cyber securities:

- *Network security*: Focuses on securing a network.
- *Application security*: Aims to secure software and devices.
- *Information security*: Protects data in storage and transit.
- *Operational security*: Focuses on processes and decisions to handle and protect data assets.
- *Disaster recovery and business continuity*: Focus on how an organization can restore its operation after any unsolicited cyber-attack.
- *End-user education*: Focuses on human factors which are one of the critical cybersecurity threats. The end user unknowingly can perform some activity that allows the intruder to insert malware into the computer and the whole network system. End-user education is critical to teach people about responding to unsolicited email attachments, plugging in an unidentified USB device, leaving their desk without locking the computer, etc.

A few cybersecurity-related precautions include:

- Software and operating systems need to be upgraded periodically.
- The use of anti-virus software is essential.
- Passwords need to be strong and unique.
- Opening of email attachments from unknown senders must be avoided.

- Opening of emails from unknown senders or unfamiliar websites must be avoided.
- Using unsecured WiFi networks in public places should be avoided.

Cybersecurity programs continue to research new defenses as cyber-criminals continuously try to create new and innovative threats.

### 6.2.2.5 Additive Manufacturing

Conventional manufacturing processes are fundamentally subtractive manufacturing (by removing materials in machines such as lathe, milling, grinding, CNC, etc.) or forming technology. The digital revolution has brought an alternate manufacturing process which is known as Additive Manufacturing (AM) or 3D Printing. Through AM, 3D objects are built by adding layer-upon-layer of material.

| | |
|---|---|
| Facilities Required for Additive Manufacturing | A computer, 3D modeling software (CAD – Computer-Aided Design), 3D Printer and Layering Material. |
| Steps for Additive Manufacturing | There are three steps for additive manufacturing where a 3D model is prepared by using CAD software. A 3D printer reads the software model and lays down successive layers of material that form the real model (Figure 6.8). |
| Layering Material | *Thermoplastics*: Thermoplastic polymers such as polycarbonate, Acrylonitrile butadiene styrene and polylactic acid are commonly used based on different applications. Water-soluble polyvinyl alcohol is generally used for creating temporary structures<br>*Metals*: Commonly used metals for 3D printing are Titanium, Aluminum, Inconel, Stainless Steel, gold or silver.<br>*Ceramic*: Zirconia, alumina and tricalcium phosphate are ceramic materials used for 3D printing.<br>*Biochemicals*: For healthcare industries use biochemical materials including silicon, calcium phosphate, etc. Another material is under exploration is bio-inks fabricated from stem cells. It will be used for creating organs such as blood vessels, bladders, etc. |
| Additive Manufacturing Technologies | *Multi-Jet Modelling (MJM)*: In MJM, additive (mostly thermoplastic) materials are sprayed layer after layer in the form of small jets. A header, capable of shuttling<br>*(Continued)* |

back and forth in x-y-z dimensions, sprayed the additive
materials such as an inkjet printer.

*Stereolithography (SLA):* In SLA, an ultraviolet (UV) laser
is focused on a vat of photopolymer resin. The UV laser
is used to draw a pre-programmed shape on the surface
of the photopolymer vat. As photopolymers are
sensitive to UV light, the resin is photochemically
solidified and forms a layer of the 3D object. Thereafter
the build platform lowers one layer and the next layer
forms. After all the layers of the 3D model are complete,
the model must be washed with a solvent to clean the
wet resin.

*Fused Filament Fabrication (FFF) or Fused Deposition
Modeling (FDM):* In FFF, a continuous filament of
thermoplastic is fed from a spool through a movable
heated printer extruder and is deposited on a growing
work.

*Selective Laser Sintering (SLS):* SLS uses a laser to sinter
powdered plastic material into a solid structure which is
based on a 3D model.

These are a few examples of additive manufacturing
technologies.

Major application areas of additive manufacturing are aerospace, automotive, healthcare and product development.

### 6.2.2.6 Artificial Intelligence

"Can machines think?" This question was raised by mathematician Alan Turing in 1950, in his paper "Computing Machinery and Intelligence." It established a vision for artificial intelligence (AI). AI is a branch of computer science that tries to explore Turing's query in the affirmative.

In a very simplistic definition, AI can be defined as building intelligent machines. However, it is too simplistic and doesn't reflect the true essence of AI. In AI, a machine has the power and logic to think, recognize and act together.

AI focuses on the following approaches (Figure 6.9):

- Thinking humanly and rationally
- Acting humanly and rationally

**FIGURE 6.8**
Additive Manufacturing Steps

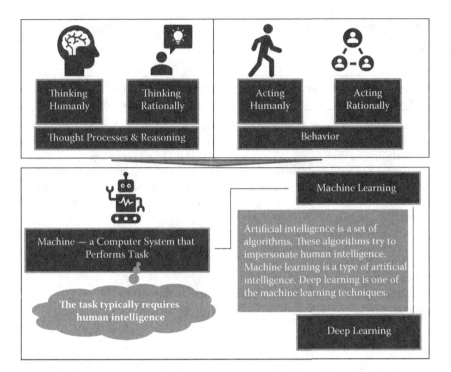

**FIGURE 6.9**
Artificial Intelligence

### Machine Learning (ML)

Machine learning is the study of computer algorithms. By use of data and through experience, these algorithms can improve automatically. This learning and performing task happen without having specifically programmed features for that particular task.

### Deep Learning (DL)

Deep Learning is a type of Machine Learning. It helps in running inputs through biologically inspired neural network architecture. The neural network is a sequence of algorithms. These algorithms are designed to identify fundamental relationships in a set of data through a process that impersonates the way the human brain operates. The neural networks are consisting of several hidden layers through which data is processed.

Narrow Artificial Intelligence and Artificial General Intelligence are two broad categories of AI.

| Narrow Artificial Intelligence (Narrow AI) Known as Weak AI | Artificial General Intelligence (AGI) Known as Strong AI or Deep AI |
|---|---|
| Some examples of Narrow AI include:<br>• Online search engines<br>• Self-driving cars<br>• Image recognition software<br>• Digital voice assistance<br><br>There are many more examples of Narrow AI, which we are accustomed to in our day-to-day lives. These have yielded significant social benefits and an economic impact globally. The focus of Narrow AI is to perform a single task extremely well. | AGI is a machine with general intelligence and it can apply intelligence to solve any problem like a human being.<br>AGI aims for a machine with a full set of cognitive abilities. The research is ongoing to develop a machine with strong AI. |

## AUGMENTED REALITY

Augmented Reality (AR) is the next thing to happen. AR connects the physical world with computer-generated digital content. AR is going to impact the business because it will be used in the product or services as well as it will be implemented in the entire business value chain. It will drastically reduce waste and cost. Also, it will increase the overall human experience and enhance the decision-making process.

### 6.2.2.7 Blockchain

For many people, blockchain means cryptocurrency. Also, for many people, blockchain means cybersecurity threats and fraudulent activities. However, blockchain is beyond all these assumptions, and is something that will change the modalities of online transaction governance in the future. Almost all businesses need an organized supply chain mechanism with legitimate verification, which can be ensured by blockchain technology. For this reason, blockchain technology is going to be used in almost all industry sectors.

A blockchain (known as Distributed Ledger Technology) is a record-keeping technology. It is a time-stamped series of incontrovertible records of the set of data or block. These data are managed online by a cluster of computers that are not owned by a single entity. Block is used to store transaction-related information such as date, time, amount, parties involved, etc. It keeps a record of the participating parties through secured approved digital signatures. Depending on pre-defined guidelines (say, the size of each block in MB) one block keeps a specific set of transaction data. Each related block is then digitally and securely connected with proper referencing by forming a chain.

Key elements of blockchain are consensus, immutability, provenance and finality.

- *Consensus*: For a transaction to be valid, the participants in the blockchain need to agree on validity. Blockchain ensures privacy of the network with encryptions along with preapproved permissions of the members which eliminate the possibility of unauthorized malicious members. The cryptographic features make the blockchain secure.
- *Immutability*: Every transaction is inconvertible. No one can tamper with a transaction once it is made, as it is recorded in an open ledger. In case of a wrong transaction, a transaction needs to be made to reverse the error. Both the transactions remain visible in a shared place.
- *Provenance*: Participants in the block are aware of the source and ownership of the asset. It restricts duplicate action on the same asset. For example, one house cannot be sold to different parties at the same time.
- *Finality*: A single shared ledger provides a single place to decide the owner of an asset and all the transactions related to that asset.
- *Smart Contracts*: A smart contract is a set of rules or agreements related to a transaction. In a blockchain, it is stored in a commonplace and executed automatically as part of a transaction. So, every time, it need not be referred to or disputed or debated between involved parties.

*What is the benefit of blockchain?*
Blockchain is important as it eliminates the deficiency of current transaction systems.

| | |
|---|---|
| Time delay occurs many a time between transaction and settlement. | ☐ In a blockchain, transactions are shared and it happens in real-time in an open environment within a defined group of participants. There is no delay between transaction and settlement. |
| Duplication of transaction calls for a third-party validation or intermediaries leading to inefficiency. | ☐ In a blockchain, transactions are shared and open. So there is no chance of duplication of a transaction for a particular purpose or entity. It eliminates the need for third-party validation or intermediaries. |
| If certain sets of transactions happen through a central system, say a bank, there are possibilities of cyberattack targeting a central source. Also, a single wrong entry can cause complexity and errors in the whole chain of transaction. | ☐ The blockchain eliminates the threat of manipulation of data. As it happens in a shared open environment and each transaction is immutable, changing a transaction is possible and the introduction of any unauthorized entity is controllable. |
| Limited transparency and inconsistency cause inefficiency in the movement of goods in the shipping industry. | ☐ The Blockchain eliminates the inefficiency with shared information. |

**FIGURE 6.10**
Benefits of Blockchain

Time delay, duplication, the possibility of cyberattacks and limited transparency are a few limitations of current transaction systems. Blockchain technologies eliminate these limitations (Figure 6.10).

Transaction volumes are increasing exponentially which will create more complexities, inefficiencies and insecurities in transaction systems. To eliminate these, the solution is the adaptation of blockchain technology.

### 6.2.3 *Ecosystem*

The business ecosystem is a network of organizations and individuals. Players within the ecosystem exchange goods and services and most importantly, information. Ecosystem players do not necessarily play traditional value chain roles. For example, at some social media apps, customers used to act as producers in an ecosystem. Companies need to change the mindset to avoid harsh competition and compete in an open environment with a cooperation model to take advantage of an ecosystem.

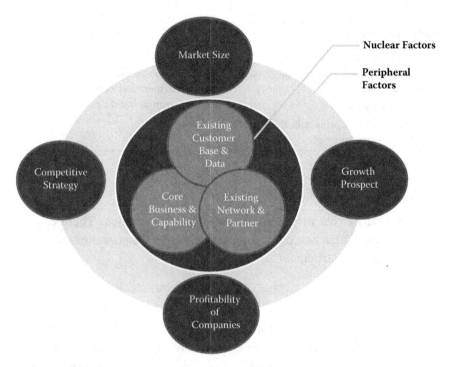

**FIGURE 6.11**
Factors for Selecting an Ecosystem

### 6.2.3.1 Factors for Selecting an Ecosystem

To decide on an ecosystem for a company, people with decision-making power should consider various nuclear and peripheral factors (Figure 6.11).

| Peripheral Factors | Nuclear Factors |
| --- | --- |
| *Market Size* | *Existing Customer Base and Data* |
| Current industry size in the ecosystem and expected penetration rate of the proposed integrated ecosystem. | A company should evaluate the availability of existing customer data. Also, it should evaluate how much customer personal data they can acquire which might be important for participating in an ecosystem. |
| *Growth Prospect* | *Core Business and Capability* |
| The projection for new customers and revenue growth. | A company should understand its core capabilities and try to evaluate the ecosystem possibilities considering its core business. |

*(Continued)*

| Peripheral Factors | Nuclear Factors |
|---|---|
| *Profitability of Companies*<br>Comparative profitability of industries in the ecosystem. | *Existing Network and Partner*<br>A company should evaluate the strength of existing partners and networks and leverage them in building an ecosystem. |
| *Competitive Strategy*<br>The strategy of competitors in the market to build a new ecosystem. | |

### 6.2.3.2 Role of the Company in an Ecosystem

The company's role in the ecosystem has to be decided. There can be three roles in which any company participates in the ecosystem: Builder, Orchestrator or Participant.

**Builder**

Ecosystem builders try to formulate a new ecosystem based on their core technology, that delivers products or services different from those available in the market. Major online commerce companies that provide e-commerce platforms to others are an example of ecosystem builders that use digital technologies to deliver new value and services to the market. In the manufacturing sector, major car manufacturers are ecosystem builders.

**Orchestrator**

Ecosystem orchestrators form a strategic partnership with companies in the value chain to offer the products or services that are already in their existing offerings. Orchestrator tries to use digital platforms to share customers and data with the members of the ecosystem.

**Participant**

Ecosystem participants act as a single link in the value chain, that offers products and services within the ecosystem.

Based on the role, a company needs to participate in the ecosystem to achieve the business objectives.

Once the role is decided, the company participates in the ecosystem by selecting a suitable business model. There can be six business models for deciding ecosystem: Acquisition engine model, Platform model, Multi-business ownership model, Data monetization model, Asset or resource synergy model and Infrastructure and capability enabler model. The company selects one of the models that suits its business objective and strategy.

| | |
|---|---|
| Acquisition engine model | Through this business model, the company can acquire new customers and maximize revenues by creating strong customer management capabilities. |
| Platform model | This business model develops digital platforms that enable participants to offer products and services. In the platform model, an orchestrator needs to have a considerably large customer base. As a participant, a company needs to utilize competitive advantages for products or services. |
| Multi-business ownership model | This model requires significant investments, as the company explores new businesses outside the scope of their core capabilities. |
| Data monetization model | This model demands advanced data and data management capabilities. Companies use collected data to develop new data-driven businesses. |
| Asset or resource synergy model | In this model, companies combine existing assets, resources and data to increase operational efficiencies and achieve business objectives. |
| Infrastructure and capability enabler model | This model allows a company to monetize current capabilities and infrastructure to decrease investment cost per unit. |

Based on the selected ecosystem model and role, the company participates in the ecosystem to achieve its business objectives. The company has to be clear about the governance of the ecosystem which sets the rules, standards and processes. Governance aims to balance value creation and value sharing. Value creation refers to rules of cooperation to create values with combined effort and value sharing depicts methodologies for distributing values among ecosystem players. It is important to take into account that the ecosystem cannot always be planned in its entirety. The ecosystem develops considering various factors. The more the governance and processes are agile and open, the more the possibility of success for the ecosystem.

## 6.2.4 Measurement

It is important for businesses to identify key parameters for return on investment, because many companies used to complain that they did not realize the intended return from a huge investment. One of the significant reasons behind this complaint is measurement of the wrong performance parameters.

A five-step approach can be useful for formulating a realistic return on investment model, which includes identifying objectives of digital transformation, defining cost centers, adopting wider view of measurement, setting realistic time scales with milestones and measuring performance continuously with consistency.

### 6.2.4.1 How to Measure Return on Investment of Digital Transformation

STEP 1: *Identifying Objectives of Digital Transformation*: The company needs to recognize the objective of adopting digital transformation. Accordingly, key performance measurement parameters of digital transformation need to be identified to suit the objective. Examples of a few of the objectives are as follows:

| | |
|---|---|
| Customer Satisfaction | Customer reviews and feedback, Order value from previous customers, number of social media mentions |
| Employee Engagement | Digital adoption, Turnover, Engagement score, Likelihood to recommend |
| Ecosystem Building | Supply chain efficiency, New collaborations, Number of new customers from new products and services, Number of new market segments |
| Technological Responsiveness | Number of innovative ideas, Proportion of new ideas implemented, Percentage of budget allocated for disruptive technologies and services |
| Operational Efficiency | Just-in-time inventory levels, Response times to emails/ chats/ phone calls, Number of interactions resolving issues on first contact, Manufacturing throughput |
| Data Security | Number of threats detected, Number of threats defended, Number of privacy breaches, Amount of losses due to fraud |

A mix of financial and nonfinancial metrics is essential to evaluate the performance of digital transformation. Instead of traditional performance matrices such as net present value (NPV) and free cash flow, there is a need for new evaluation approaches. For example, while calculating NPV, life cycle thinking should be introduced, which will consider diminishing returns from an existing business if it is in the decline phase. Also, investment in digital technologies increases options for the business in an uncertain market. With the use of options thinking, companies can create an opportunity portfolio, which is essential to evaluate a business's need for digital transformation.

STEP 2: *Defining Cost Centers*: It is not recommended to assign all digital transformation-related costs to the IT department. Digital transformation should be effectively implemented in all the business functions. So key performance measurement parameters for the cost centers should be identified so that the effect of digital transformation can be measured at a micro-level.

STEP 3: *Adopting Wider View of Measurement*: One of the major purposes of digital transformation is enhancing customer experience which eventually will help in revenue generation in long term. So while finalizing the key measurement parameters, it is important to include those parameters that have a direct impact on revenue, such as satisfaction score, repeated purchase data, referrals, etc. Measuring these values provides a wider view regarding the impact of digital transformation on customer experience.

STEP 4: *Setting Realistic Time Scales with Milestones*: While finalizing the key performance parameters, it is also recommended to identify over what period all the parameters to be monitored. The duration of the monitor may vary for different parameters.

STEP 5: *Measuring Performance Continuously with Consistency*: This is required to measure and monitor the identified parameters continuously as per plan. It clarifies how each performance parameter affects the overall return on investment. Based on the measured data, cause and effect analyses are undertaken to understand business performance. This analysis helps a business to identify and effectively address potential concerns.

Digital transformation is inevitable for the sustainability of a business. While adopting digital transformation, businesses need to track return on investment appropriately to avoid any post-investment dilemma. These five steps may be useful for measuring the effect of digital transformation and return on investment, holistically (Figure 6.12).

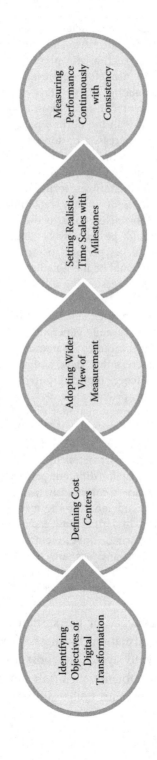

**FIGURE 6.12**
Steps of Measuring Return on Investment of Digital Transformation

## HOW TO INVEST IN AN AMBIDEXTROUS SCENARIO?

How much is necessary to invest in an ambidextrous environment to maintain a balance between exploration and exploitation? Honestly, it is a million-dollar question. In a stable classical environment if the company decided to invest say 10 per cent of the total investment for exploration and remaining in exploitation, then more homework is needed in an uncertain dynamic market scenario. Also, a strong feedback mechanism is necessary to monitor and control the investment. If the digital growth team comes up with great ideas and prototypes in a shorter time frame, maybe the next investment can be increased to a certain portion, say 15 per cent. However, if the prototype or the idea fails in the trial, probably the further investment needs to be reduced again to 10 per cent or maybe less. So, depending on the situation, the investment pattern must be flexible and adjustable.

## LOOKING FOR AN EXCITING FUTURE: AN INTERVIEW WITH CLAIRE OATWAY, BUSINESS STRATEGIST FROM THE UNITED KINGDOM

Claire Oatway is a business advisor and consultant. Starting her career as Intelligence Analyst and Data Specialist for Kent Police in 1996, she served in various business sectors including healthcare. Claire was Clinical Advisor at NHS England where her role was to help Primary Care Networks to develop multidisciplinary teams. In 2020, she founded business management consultancy, Neon Juno to help strategic leaders and entrepreneurs with strategy, change management and leadership development.

**Is digital transformation a must for companies that are still "lagging in adopting digital?"**

*Claire:* Digital has to be in the DNA for companies now. Even if not through a massive transformation there is still opportunity for evolution. It isn't too late and we've seen in global markets that late adopters can leapfrog competitors who didn't have a clear strategy on implementation.

Change is accelerating indeed and new technologies are being introduced at a faster pace than ever before. This means that even those who have already invested need to upgrade again and again. The keyword is transformation. That doesn't mean incremental change or a tweak here or there. It required a new thought process and a new way of work. Digital is the tool that supports transformation which is a step change in how a business operates.

**In the digital era, what are some of the challenges faced by the industry?**

*Claire:* Digital skills and literacy are likely to be a limiting factor. It can be foreseen that the next decade will be characterized by the need for hybrid digital and nondigital support for people. There are generational and culture divides in terms of technological adoption and many firms will need to invest in both areas for some time yet.

Similarly, one of the strategy errors happening around automation is to directly substitute human roles for digital processes. While formulating the strategy there is a need to understand the value of humans in processes. Organizations should look for additional value that humans can bring to the process – the relationship aspects perhaps. Wherever possible, strategy needs to be formulated considering technology and humans together not either or.

Digital tools can be used to enhance roles. If an organization is only looking at the cost argument and lost hours it may become more efficient but lose the opportunity for growth.

**It is said that digital has increased customer centricity for businesses, how so?**

*Claire:* We have been coming out of an era where competitive advantage was found in tighter supply chain management and efficiencies. In many industries, the focus on price and profit has weakened relationships to the point of transactions.

It's true that to differentiate and to retain customers, many businesses have started deploying User Experience (UX) in design and driving up value in the eyes of consumers.

Many consumers now want both high value and low cost. Of course, digital can provide that. A few e-commerce companies are trying to help customers buy cheaper goods and more goods.

One of the most progressive leaps has been in the accumulation and use of data. Digital gives most industries incredible levels of insight into their customer's buying and consumption habits. The use of data can build trust and improve repeat purchases. The data can help inform market expansion with lookalike audiences, and most innovatively can identify product or service variations that appear highly tailored to the consumer.

Finally, digital afforded visibility to businesses through the Internet and social media. Any business that has a website is now international. This means that competition for buyers' attention is intense. Firms need to differentiate to retain relationships. Visibility also means that buyers have increased power and influence on others. Complaints leveraged through online comparison or social media have more credence and reach than in a traditional community. Firms need to be responsive to that. This increased responsiveness does bring increased customer centricity.

**How is strategy important in the digital era? What is the future of strategy?**

*Claire:* There are examples where business strategy and digital strategy are often detached. Many public sectors and corporate houses implement digital projects in isolation from operations and human resource activities. In the digital era, this is not the right approach. There is a need for amalgamation between business strategy and digital strategy.

Businesses are human systems. A business is a group of humans led by humans to serve other humans. When a business expands by participating in an ecosystem, it adds in more and more humans.

Humans bring complexity – they bring emotion. Even when humans behave in groups, they add an element of unpredictability. Therefore, the strategy will always have a place to analyze and identify behavior patterns then recommend and steer action. No algorithm on the planet can do that independently.

The "purpose" is becoming increasingly important in the face of scarce resources and social needs. There are disruptions to marketplaces where firms look to create their network effect. To connect to an idea that a business doesn't need to be as big as an independent player. It can leverage a network effect by building communities around it. A natural interdependence between firms and leaders can create new markets and opportunities.

In the digital era, there is a need to distribute ownership and innovation throughout the organization. It calls for a new breed of leader. Transformational leadership is important. Humility and action orientation will become very important in the future. The key to being agile will be to harness the collective strength of employees and other stakeholders.

### Where are we going from here into the future?

*Claire:* The future will be an era where nothing is guaranteed. The competitive advantage will come from building a system that thrives and strengthens when under pressure and acts within an ecosystem.

The scarcity of resources due to climate change and the unsettled supply chains will call for the true nature of global interdependence.

The future will redefine the coexistence of humans and machines. There will be new ways that humans will add value. There are so many big problems to solve together!

It will be an exciting future where humans and machines will effectively work in unison!

Digital will redefine the way of life!

# 7

## *Life Cycle Benefits*

Digital technologies have made an enormous impact which is having cascading effect. It has created profound opportunities and serious challenges to all aspects of society and business.

The exponential growth in data capacity (storage, process and communication) has provided infinite business prospects and added new dimensions to the business. Digital platforms have developed alternative business models by deconstructing the traditional value chains. Agile concepts driven by design thinking have brought innovative perspectives that have created an environment of boundless disruption. To run a company with sustainability and manage disruptions more consciously, adopting a digital platform with an appropriate strategy is the only viable option.

Each company has its own digital transformation (DX) goal and strategy in line with its business objective. A successful digital transformation creates varied benefits to businesses depending on the framework and implementation strategy. Company leadership plays a significant role to bring stakeholders into a common platform to maximize the benefit of the DX process. The common benefits of digital transformation for companies are improved customer experience, improved operational efficiency, differentiated product and service offerings, innovative business models and reduced business risk (Figure 7.1).

DOI: 10.4324/9781003270904-7

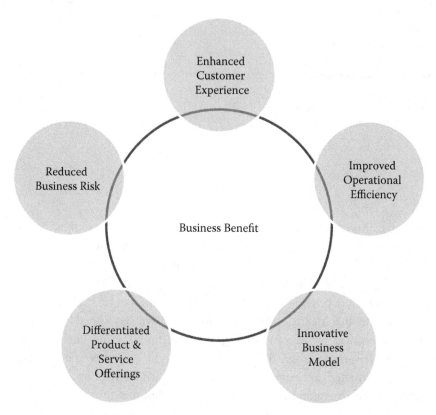

**FIGURE 7.1**
Benefits of Digital Transformation

## 7.1 LIFE CYCLE BENEFITS OF STRATEGIC STRUCTURE COMPONENTS

The traditional or legacy business model focuses on improving internal capabilities to maximize profit, whereas the digital transformation has brought the customer into center stage. Digital transformation has opened avenues for businesses to improve sustainability in terms of company and customer journeys. The digital platform not only focuses on delivering the end product to customers, rather it has taken the customer on a journey by enhancing the customer experience. Starting from product development to continuous improvement, customers have become part of a company's business. The companies that are effectively taking advantage of the digital platform to enhance customer experience are sustainably maneuvering through the highly disruptive business environment. Tactical implementation of various components of strategic structure helps a company in this transformational journey (Figure 7.2).

The strategic structure is not a ready-to-use recipe for implementing the digital transformation process, but rather a general guide. Also, it is not a step-by-step approach. A company should work simultaneously on various elements of the strategic structure based on objectives and business strategy. It must be remembered that each company is different and that the amount of digitalization for a company is tailored. It may

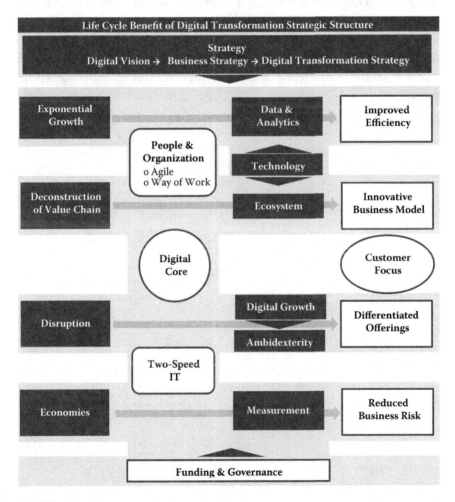

**FIGURE 7.2**
Life Cycle Benefits Model

happen that a company has already taken some initiatives for digital transformation. In this context, the company must work on strategic structure elements that are not yet explored. It will help to adopt a consolidated approach to maximize the benefits of digitalization.

Like any other transformational process, digital transformation has created a structural tension between "old" and "new." In this tension, employees have a large role to play, whose clarity of thought regarding the transformation process is of paramount interest. To overcome this tension, the organization needs to orient itself as a learning organization, which will create opportunities for growth in an ambidextrous environment, embraced with a digital ecosystem.

Because of digital transformation, the world is changing very fast, and therefore the business models. Adapting to change through digital transformation is not just a mantra of survival, but also a roadmap to success.

# References

ABB, 2019. *ABB Ability™ AssetVista Condition Monitoring for Metals.* [Online] Available at: https://search.abb.com/library/Download.aspx?DocumentID=9AKK107492A7323& LanguageCode=en&DocumentPartId=&Action=Launch [Accessed 15 July 2020].

Accenture, 2018. *Disruption Need Not Be an Enigma.* [Online] Available at: https:// www.accenture.com/us-en/insight-leading-new-disruptability-index [Accessed 11 July 2020].

Accenture, 2020. *Together Makes Better – How to Drive Cross-Function Collaboration.* [Online] Available at: https://www.accenture.com/_acnmedia/Thought-Leadership-Assets/PDF-3/Accenture-IndustryX0-Out-Collaborate-the-Crisis-v3.pdf#zoom=50 [Accessed 11 July 2020].

Atlassian, n.d. *The Agile Coach.* [Online] Available at: https://www.atlassian.com/agile [Accessed 22 July 2020].

BCG, n.d. *Achieving Agile at Scale.* [Online] Available at: https://www.bcg.com/en-be/ digital-bcg/agile/large-scale-agile-transformation [Accessed 22 July 2020].

Berman, J., 2020. *Agile at Scale.* [Online] Available at: https://www.atlassian.com/agile/ agile-at-scale [Accessed 24 August 2020].

Bossert, O., Ip, C. & Laartz, J., 2014. *A Two-Speed IT Architecture for the Digital Enterprise.* [Online] Available at: https://www.mckinsey.com/business-functions/mckinsey-digital/our-insights/a-two-speed-it-architecture-for-the-digital-enterprise [Accessed 16 August 2020].

Boston Consulting Group, 2020. *Enabling Digital Transformation with BCG's Data & Digital Platform.* [Online] Available at: https://www.bcg.com/capabilities/digital-technology-data/digital-platform [Accessed 02 September 2020].

Branca, T. A. et al., 2020, February 21. The Challenge of Digitalization in the Steel Sector. *Metals, 10*(2). 10.3390/met10020288

Builtin, 2020. *Artificial Intelligence.* [Online] Available at: https://builtin.com/artificial-intelligence [Accessed 20 September 2020].

Cognition Agency, 2020. *Digital Thinking.* [Online] Available at: https://www. cognitionagency.co.uk/about-us/digital-thinking [Accessed 18 July 2020].

Deloitte, 2013. *The Digital Transformation of Customer Services.* [Online] Available at: https://www2.deloitte.com/content/dam/Deloitte/nl/Documents/consumer-business/deloitte-nl-the-digital-transformation-of-customer-services.pdf [Accessed 24 September 2020].

Denecken, S., 2015. *Digitize the Core to Manage the Digital Transformation.* [Online] Available at: https://www.zdnet.com/article/digitize-the-core-to-manage-the-digital-transformation/ [Accessed 03 August 2020].

DiSalvo, D., 2013. *Your Brain Sees Even When You Don't.* [Online] Available at: https://www.forbes.com/sites/daviddisalvo/2013/06/22/your-brain-sees-even-when-you-dont/#2f201822116a [Accessed 08 July 2020].

Engage Hub, 2018. *Digital Transformation, Customer Experience & Calculating ROI.* London: Engage Hub.

European Commission, 2015. *Development of Tools for Reduction of Energy Demand and $CO_2$-emissions within the Iron and Steel Industry Based on Energy Register, $CO_2$-Monitoring and Waste Heat Power Generation (ENCOP).* Brussels: European Commission.

European Commission, 2018. *Digital Transformation Scoreboard 2018.* Luxembourg: European Union.

Gallup, 2018. *The Real Future of Work.* [Online] Available at: https://www.gallup.com/workplace/241295/future-work-agility-download.aspx [Accessed 20 August 2020].

Garratt, M., 2018. *Why Disruption Is Coming for Your Industry – And How to Embrace It.* [Online] Available at: https://www.entrepreneur.com/article/324260 [Accessed 11 July 2020].

Gartner, 2017. *8 Dimensions of Business Ecosystems.* [Online] Available at: https://www.gartner.com/smarterwithgartner/8-dimensions-of-business-ecosystems/

Gartner, 2019. *Why Data and Analytics Are Key to Digital Transformation.* [Online] Available at: https://www.gartner.com/smarterwithgartner/why-data-and-analytics-are-key-to-digital-transformation/ [Accessed 26 July 2020].

General Electric, 2020. *What Is Additive Manufacturing?* [Online] Available at: https://www.ge.com/additive/additive-manufacturing [Accessed 19 September 2020].

Godin, V. V. & Terekhova, A. E., 2020. *Digital Ecosystems as a Form of Modern Business Transformation,* Moscow, Russia: ICID-2019 Conference.

Gupta, M., 2020. *Blockchain for Dummies.* [Online] Available at: https://www.ibm.com/downloads/cas/OK5M0E49 [Accessed 20 September 2020].

Guru99, 2020. *Scrum vs. Kanban: Know the Difference.* [Online] Available at: https://www.guru99.com/scrum-vs-kanban.html#:~:text=Scrum%20is%20an%20agile%20process%20that%20allows%20us%20to%20focus,for%20managing%20software%20development%20work.&text=amongst%20them%20all.-,Scrum%20prescribes%20time%2Dboxed%20iterations.,different%2 [Accessed 24 August 2020].

Herzog, K., 2017. *The Way to Digitalized Steel Production.* Ijmuiden: Primetals Technologies Austria GmbH.

IDC, 2019. *Worldwide Spending on Digital Transformation Will Reach $2.3 Trillion in 2023.* [Online] Available at: https://www.idc.com/getdoc.jsp?containerId=prUS45612419 [Accessed 01 July 2020].

Infosys Public Services, 2015. *Two-Speed IT.* [Online] Available at: https://www.infosyspublicservices.com/industries/public-sector/perspectives/Documents/two-speed-IT.pdf [Accessed 31 August 2020].

IoT For All, 2020. *What Is IoT? A Simple Explanation of the Internet of Things.* [Online] Available at: https://www.iotforall.com/what-is-iot-simple-explanation/ [Accessed 17 September 2020].

Ismail, N., 2018. *Companies Are Wasting Millions on Digital Investment Because They Are Measuring the Wrong KPI.* [Online] Available at: https://www.information-age.com/companies-wasting-millions-digital-investment-123471707/ [Accessed 12 July 2020].

Kaspersky, 2020. *What Is Cyber Security?* [Online] Available at: https://www.kaspersky.com/resource-center/definitions/what-is-cyber-security [Accessed 20 September 2020].

Ketterer, H., Rehberg, B. & Schmid, C., 2016. *The End of Two-Speed IT.* [Online] Available at: https://www.bcg.com/publications/2016/software-agile-digital-transformation-end-of-two-speed-it [Accessed 16 August 2020].

Kylliäinen, J., 2019. *Types of Innovation – The Ultimate Guide with Definitions and Examples.* [Online] Available at: https://www.viima.com/blog/types-of-innovation?_ga=2.119923400.1144220331.1574844302-1577955596.1567515276 [Accessed 31 August 2020].

Max, R. & Ritchie, H., 2013. Technological Progress. *Our World in Data.* https://ourworldindata.org/technological-progress.

Mazumdar, R., 2018. *Tata Steel Launches New Website, Aashiyana.* Kolkata: The Economic Times.

McKinsey & Company, 2019. *The Ecosystem Playbook: Winning in a World of Ecosystems.* [Online] Available at: https://www.mckinsey.com/~/media/mckinsey/industries/financial%20services/our%20insights/winning%20in%20a%20world%20of%20eco-systems/winning-in-a-world-of-ecosystems-vf.ashx [Accessed 08 September 2020].

Microsoft Azure, 2020. *What Is Cloud Computing?* [Online] Available at: https://azure.microsoft.com/en-us/overview/what-is-cloud-computing/#benefits [Accessed 16 September 2020].

Mühleisen, M., 2018, June. The Long and Short of the Digital Revolution. *Finance & Development, 55*(2), p. 4.

MuleSoft, LLC, 2020. *B2B/EDI: Modern Supply Chain Management.* [Online] Available at: https://www.mulesoft.com/ty/wp/supply-chain-management-edi-system?utm_source=google&utm_medium=cpc&utm_campaign=g-asset-uki-search-supply-chain&utm_term=supply%20chain&utm_content=g-p-c&gclid=CjwKCAjwr7X4BRA4EiwAUXjbt-gZJoWrLjAAY67xaHFT71s3RBqFAKddgR9urRe [Accessed 15 July 2020].

Nieto-Rodriguez, A., 2014. *Organisational Ambidexterity.* [Online] Available at: https://www.london.edu/think/organisational-ambidexterity [Accessed 09 August 2020].

Nintex, 2020. *Three Steps to Digitizing Your Core Business Processes.* [Online] Available at: https://www.nintex.com/blog/digitize-core-business-processes/ [Accessed 03 August 2020].

Nischak, F. & Hanelt, A., 2019. *Ecosystem Change in the Era of Digital Innovation – A Longitudinal Analysis and Visualization of the Automotive Ecosystem.* Munich: International Conference on Information Systems.

Novacek, G. et al., 2017. *Organizing for a Digital Future.* [Online] Available at: https://www.bcg.com/en-be/publications/2017/technology-organizing-for-digital-future [Accessed 22 August 2020].

O'Reilly III, C. A. & Tushman, M. L., 2004. *The Ambidextrous Organization.* [Online] Available at: https://hbr.org/2004/04/the-ambidextrous-organization [Accessed 08 August 2020].

OECD, 2018. *Implications of the Digital Transformation for the Business Sector.* London: Organisation for Economic Co-operation and Development (OECD).

Oracle, 2020. *What Is Big Data?* [Online] Available at: https://www.oracle.com/big-data/what-is-big-data.html [Accessed 17 September 2020].

Pidun, U. & Reeves, M., 2020. *How Do You "Design" a Business Ecosystem?* [Online] Available at: https://www.bcg.com/en-be/publications/2020/how-do-you-design-a-business-ecosystem [Accessed 11 September 2020].

Prising, J., Sorenson, A. & Weinelt, B., 2018. *Maximizing the Return on Digital Investments.* Geneva: World Economic Forum.

PTC, Inc., 2019. *The State of Industrial Digital Transformation.* [Online] Available at: https://www.ptc.com/-/media/Files/PDFs/IoT/State-of-Digital-Transformation-whitepaper.pdf [Accessed 11 September 2020].

PWC, 2016. *What's Your Digital ROI?* [Online] Available at: https://www.strategyand.pwc.com/ca/en/media/whats-your-digital-roi.pdf [Accessed 11 July 2020].

Reeves, M., Deimler, M. & Love, C., 2012. *Why Strategy Needs a Strategy.* [Online] Available at: https://www.bcg.com/en-be/publications/2012/why-strategy-needs-a-strategy.aspx

Reeves, M., Haanæs, K., Hollingsworth, J. & Scognamiglio, F., 2013. *Ambidexterity: The Art of Thriving in Complex Environments.* [Online] Available at: https://www.bcg.com/en-be/publications/2013/strategy-growth-ambidexterity-art-thriving-complex-environments [Accessed 10 August 2020].

Rouse, M., 2014. *Kryder's Law.* [Online] Available at: https://searchstorage.techtarget.com/definition/Kryders-Law [Accessed 07 July 2020].

S&P and MSCI, 2018. *Global Industry Classification Standard.* [Online] Available at: https://www.spglobal.com/marketintelligence/en/documents/112727-gics-mapbook_2018_v3_letter_digitalspreads.pdf

Shalf, J. & Leland, R., 2015. Computing beyond Moore's Law. *Computer*, 48(12), pp. 14–23.

Shee, A., Turvey, C. G. & Marr, A., 2019. *Heterogeneous Demand and Supply for an Insurance-Linked Credit Product in Kenya: A Stated Choice Experiment Approach.* Atlanta: Agricultural & Applied Economics Association.

Smith, C., 2017. *The Importance of Data in Manufacturing.* [Online] Available at: https://www.monarchmetal.com/blog/the-importance-of-data-in-manufacturing/#:~:text=Data%2Ddriven%20manufacturing%20allows%20management,the%20mainstays%20of%20the%20business. [Accessed 08 July 2020].

SMS Group, 2017. *Digitalization in the Steel Industry.* [Online] Available at: https://www.sms-group.com/sms-group-magazine/overview/digitalization-in-the-steel-industry/ [Accessed 15 July 2020].

Stern, C. W., 1998. *The Deconstruction of Value Chains.* [Online] Available at: https://image-src.bcg.com/Images/Eng372-The_Deconstruction_ofValue_chains_tcm89-138894.pdf [Accessed 08 July 2020].

Tabrizi, B., Lam, E., Girard, K. & Irvin, V., 2019. *Digital Transformation Is Not about Technology.* [Online] Available at: https://hbr.org/2019/03/digital-transformation-is-not-about-technology [Accessed 28 January 2022].

Talin, V. B., 2019. *Exponential Change due to Exponential Growth.* [Online] Available at: https://morethandigital.info/en/exponential-change-due-exponential-growth/ [Accessed 03 July 2020].

Wald, D., Laubier, R. d. & Charanya, T., 2019. *The Five Rules of Digital Strategy.* [Online] Available at: https://www.bcg.com/en-be/publications/2019/five-rules-digital-strategy.aspx [Accessed 28 January 2022].

World Economic Forum, 2016. *Digital Transformation of Industries.* Geneva: World Economic Forum.

World Economic Forum, 2017. *Digital Transformation Initiative – Mining and Metals Industry.* Geneva: World Economic Forum.

Wyck, J. V. et al., 2019. *Organizing for Digital Operations at Scale.* [Online] Available at: https://www.bcg.com/en-be/publications/2019/digital-operations-at-scale [Accessed 17 August 2020].

Xu, M., David, J. M. & Kim, S. H., 2018. The Fourth Industrial Revolution: Opportunities and Challenges. *International Journal of Financial Research*, 9(2), p. 90. 10.5430/ijfr.v9n2p90

Zhou, Y. & Hu, L., 2019. *The Digital Revolution Will Transform the Steel Industry.* [Online] Available at: https://www.weforum.org/agenda/2019/06/the-digital-revolution-will-transform-steel-and-metals-companies/ [Accessed 15 July 2020].

# Index

Page numbers followed by "f" indicate figures; page numbers followed by "t" indicate tables.

acquisition engine model, 85
adaptability, digital thinking, 26
additive manufacturing (AM), 76–7; steps, 76, 78f
Adware, 74
AGI. *See* artificial general intelligence
agile approach, 28–9, 33; agile scale, 49–55; customers and, 52; empiricism and, 51; features, 49; in IT industry, 53–4; Mukherjee on, 50–1; non-software projects and, 53–4; trio, 43–7; value delivery, 50–5; *vs.* traditional, 51–2, 53
AI. *See* artificial intelligence
AM. *See* additive manufacturing
Amberg, Germany, 16
ambidexterity, 35–9; components of, 35, 35f; digital growth with, 60–1; exploration and exploitation, 35–9; investment and, 89; promoting ambidextrous business, 36–9, 37f.
*See also* framework, digital transformation
Apache Hadoop, 70
Apache Spark, 70
API. *See* Application Programming Interface
applicability, digital transformation, 15–21, 16f
Application Programming Interface (API), 64
application security, 75
AR. *See* augmented reality
artificial general intelligence (AGI), 80
artificial intelligence (AI), 14, 77–80, 79f; approaches, 77, 79f; artificial general intelligence, 80; defined, 77; narrow AI, 80

asset or resource synergy model, 85
augmented reality (AR), 80
automation, 18.
*See also* digital transformation

BDA. *See* big data analysis
Big Data, 67–70; five Vs, 69
big data analysis (BDA), 14
BIM. *See* Building Information Modelling
blockchain, 80–2, 82f; benefits, 81–2, 82f; elements of, 81
BU. *See* business unit
builders, ecosystem, 84
Building Information Modelling (BIM), 16
business unit (BU), 47
Butter's law, 8

CAD. *See* computer-aided design
capability delivery activities: enabler delivery, 57, 58f, 65–92; overview, 57, 58f; process delivery, 57–64, 58f; purpose, 57
capability delivery components, 29–31; data and analytics, 29–30; ecosystem, 30–1; technology, 30
CDO. *See* Chief Digital Officer
centralized model, 47, 48f
Chief Digital Officer (CDO), 47
Cloud, 2, 20, 70–2; advantages, 70–1
collaboration, digital thinking, 26
communicating, data, 8
computer-aided design (CAD), 76
connectivity, 18
consensus, blockchain and, 81
consistency, 87, 88f
construction industry, digitization, 16
co-opetition, 1, 30
cost, Cloud computing, 70

cost, digitally advanced equipment, 8
cost centers, 87, 88f
cross-selling, 40
cryptocurrency, 80.
    *See also* blockchain
customer expectations, 32, 39
customer-centric culture, 47
customer centricity, 90–1
cybersecurities, 73–6
cyberthreats, 74–6; categories, 73–4
cyberattack, 82, 82f
cybercrime, 73
cybercriminals, 74
cyberterrorism, 74

data analysis, 65
Data Analytics, 65
data and analytics, 29–30, 65
data monetization model, 85
data policy, 66–7
data-driven manufacturing, 8–9, 29
decentralized model, 47, 48f, 49
deep AI, 80
deep learning (DL), 79
denial-of-service attack, 75
digital challenges for industries, 5, 6f
digital core, 31–2
Digital Customer Access model, 18
digital data, 17
digital duality, 31–4
digital growth, 32–3; steps for, 33, 33f
digital thinking, 25–6
digital transformation, 34, 34f;
        applicability of, 15–21, 16f;
        benefits, 93, 94f; challenges, 90;
        due to general-purpose
        technologies, 1; framework,
        23–42, 24f; goals, 93; identifying
        objectives of, 86–7, 88f; impact
        of, 1–2; Oatway, Claire, on,
        89–90; overview, 1–3; purpose
        of, 2; strategic structure, 2f, 3
digital vision, 26–7
digitalization, 34, 34f
digitization, 34, 34f
disaster recovery and business
        continuity, 75
disruption, 11–13; defined, 12

Distributed Ledger Technology, 81.
    *See also* blockchain
DL. *See* deep learning
doubling phenomenon, 7
duplication, 82, 82f

EBO. *See* Emerging Business Organization
economic benefit, implementation, 13–14
ecosystem, 30–1, 82–5; acquisition engine
        model, 85; asset or resource
        synergy model, 85; company's
        role in, 84–5; data monetization
        model, 85; factors for selecting,
        83–4, 83f; infrastructure and
        capability enabler model, 85;
        multi-business ownership
        model, 85; nuclear factors, 83–4;
        peripheral factors, 83–4;
        platform model, 85
electronics plant, digitization, 16
emerging business, separation
        approach, 36–7
Emerging Business Organization
        (EBO), 37
empiricism, agile and, 51
employee participation, 46–7
enabler delivery, 57, 58f, 65–92; data and
        analytics, 65–7; ecosystem, 82–5;
        measurement, 86–7, 88f;
        technology, 67–80.
        *See also* technology, capability
        delivery and
end-user education, 75
ethics, data policy and, 67
excubator model, 48f, 49
experimentation, digital thinking, 25–6
exploitation, 35–9, 35f.
        *See also* ambidexterity
exploration, 35–9, 35f.
        *See also* ambidexterity
exponential growth, digital technologies,
        5–9, 93; Butter's law, 8; Kryder's
        law, 8; Moore's law, 7–8

fifth-generation wireless mobile network
        (5G), 73
finality, blockchain and, 81
five-step approach, measurement, 86–7

flexibility, Cloud computing, 70
flow diagram automation, 59
food industry, digitization, 17
framework, digital transformation, 23–42,
 24f; ambidexterity, 35–9;
 capability delivery components,
 29–31; digital duality, 31–4;
 digital vision, 26–7; ecosystem,
 31; enabling factors, 27–31;
 people and organizations, 27–9;
 strategy, 23–6
funding and governance, 41–2

general-purpose technologies, 1
GICS. *See* Global Industry Classification
 Standard
Global Industry Classification Standard
 (GICS), 15
governance and funding, 41–2

Hadoop, 67
Halloran, David G., Dr., 19–21
Halloran Associates, 19–21
high-speed IT team, 62, 64, 64f
horizontally stacked value chain, 10–11,
 11f, 28.
 *See also* value chain
hotel industry, digitization, 16–17
hybrid model, 48f, 49

IaaS. *See* Infrastructure as a Service
immutability, blockchain and, 81
incumbent business, 11–13
Industrial Revolution, 12, 12f
Industry 4.0 Revolution, 5, 12, 13, 19, 26
industry-specific digital initiatives, 19t
information, 8
information security, 75
infrastructure and capability enabler
 model, 85
Infrastructure as a Service (IaaS), 71
innovation, 27, 28, 39
Innovation Chart, 60, 61f
Innovation Matrix, 61f
Insurance-Linked Credit, 17
interconnection, 18
Internet of Things (IoT), 2, 8, 14, 17, 72–3;
 benefits, 72–3; components, 72

interviews: Halloran, David G., Dr., 19–21;
 Mukherjee, Samik, 50–5;
 Oatway, Claire, 89–92
IoT. *See* Internet of Things

Jenus (Roman mythology), 35

Keynes, Maynard, Dr., 19
Kryder's law, 8

leadership, 44–5, 45f; transformational,
 45–6, 46f
legacy business: digital growth, 32;
 separation approach, 36
legacy IT system: architecture, 39–41;
 high-speed IT and, integration,
 62, 64, 64f
life cycle benefits, 93–6
limited transparency, 82, 82f

machine learning (ML), 89
malleability, 23.
 *See also* strategy
malware (malicious software), 74
man-in-the-middle attack, 75
manufacturing sector, digitization:
 Halloran, David G., on, 21;
 processing, communicating and
 storing, 8–9
manufacturing sectors, decision-making
 dilemma, 5
market disruption, 11–13
measurement, 86–7, 88f; five-step
 approach, 86–7
MJM. *See* multi-jet modelling
ML. *See* machine learning
mobile networks, 73
Moore, Gordon, 7
Moore's law, 7–8
Mukherjee, Samik, 50–5
multi-business ownership model, 85
multi-jet modelling (MJM), 76

network generation, 73
network security, 75
nuclear factors, ecosystem, 83–4

Oatway, Claire, 89–92

omnichannel retail, 17
operational security, 75
orchestrators, ecosystem, 84
organizational culture, 27–8
organizational structure models, 47–9, 48f;
    centralized, 47; decentralized, 47,
    49; excubator, 49; hybrid,
    47, 49

PaaS. *See* Platform as a Service
participants, ecosystem, 84
people and organizations, 27–9
people engagement in organizational
    process, 43, 44f
performance, Cloud computing and, 71
performance measurement, 87, 88f
peripheral factors, ecosystem, 83–4
phishing, 74
Platform as a Service (PaaS), 71
platform model, 85
predictability, 23.
    *See also* strategy
process delivery, 57–64, 58f; digital growth
    with ambidexterity, 60–1, 61f;
    digitize core, 58–60, 59f; two-
    speed IT, 61–4, 63f
process flow diagram creation, 58–9
processing, data, 8
productivity, Cloud computing and, 71
provenance, blockchain and, 81
pyramid, digital, 34, 34f

ransomware, 74
realistic time scales, 87, 88f
reliability, Cloud computing and, 71
resource synergy model, 85
robotic process automation (RPA), 60
robotics, 14
RPA. *See* robotic process automation

SaaS. *See* Software as a Service (SaaS)
scaling: agile, 49–55; Cloud computing
    and, 70
scaling phenomenon, 7
*Scientific American* (journal), 8
security, Cloud computing, 71
sensors, 72

separation approach, 36–7
serverless computing model, 72
shrinking dimension, 7
simplicity, digital thinking, 25
Software as a Service (SaaS), 71
Solow, Robert, 13
Solow's Paradox, 13
Spark, 67
speed, digital thinking, 25
spending on digital transformation, 15
spyware, 74
SQL injection, 74
steel and metal industry, digitization,
    17–18, 18f
storing, data, 8
strategic structure: life cycle benefit of,
    94–6, 95f; overview, 2f, 3
strategy: consideration of, 23; digital
    vision, 26–7; framework and,
    23–6; importance of, 91–2;
    malleability, 23; Oatway, Claire,
    on, 89–92; predictability, 23
strong AI, 80
switching approach, 37–8

technology, capability delivery and, 30,
    67–82, 68f; additive
    manufacturing, 76–7; artificial
    intelligence, 14, 77–80, 79f; Big
    Data, 67–70; blockchain, 80–2,
    82f; Cloud, 2, 20, 70–2;
    cybersecurities, 73–6; IoT, 2, 8,
    14, 17, 72–3
technology, digital. *See* digital
    transformation
test-fail-learn-adapt-iterate approach, 40–1
thermoplastic polymers, 76
3D scanning, 16
time delay, 82, 82f
transaction, 31–2
transformational leadership, 45–6, 46f
Trojans, 74
Turing, Alan, 77
2020 Global Survey Report, 13
2D lithography, 7
two-speed IT, 39–41, 61–4, 63f;
    implementation approach, 62

User Experience (UX), 90

value, Big Data and, 69
value chain: deconstruction of, 9–11;
  horizontally stacked value chain,
  10–11, 11f; vertically stacked,
  9, 10f
value delivery, agile approach and, 50–5
variety, Big Data and, 69
velocity, Big Data and, 69
veracity, Big Data and, 69

vertically stacked value chain, 9, 10f.
  *See also* value chain
virtual machines (VMs), 71
virus, 74
VMs. *See* virtual machines
volume, Big Data and, 69

way of work (WoW), 43, 49
WoW. *See* way of work

"zero-defect" quality goal, 17

Printed in the United States
by Baker & Taylor Publisher Services